Grit and Spit:
The Dirty Truth of Academia

A collection of essays from students, faculty, and alumni at Northwest Missouri State University

Publication Skills 10-512-01
Northwest Missouri State University
Maryville, Missouri

2013

Grit and Spit
The Dirty Truth of Academia

Introduction: Richard Sonnenmoser
Editors: Shea Boughton, Kate Dittmann, Katie Hardisty, Karlee Liberty, Taylor Mothershead, Chelsea Nichols, Alyssa Striplin, Clayton Stuart, Mara Wilson
Cover Art: Justin Bruss
Cover Design: Kate Dittmann

Special thanks to the Office of the Provost and the Improvement of Teaching and Learning Committee for making this project possible.

Table of Contents

Introduction	Richard Sonnenmoser	4
Time to Get Gritty: The Non-Academic Stuff that Makes You a Better Student	Kori Binette	9
A Class I Learned From	Shea Boughton	12
Acadakid Transitions	Samantha Compton	17
My Wake-Up Call	Kate Dittmann	20
How to Find Your Niche	Sarah Dittmann	24
The Value of a College Education	Yahaya Gwamna	27
Community Changing	Katie Hardisty	29
Your Major is Not Your Only Place	Kara Huen	31
A Week in the Life	Karlee Liberty	33
Finding Friends	Taylor Mothershead	36
The Art of Juggling	Chelsea Nichols	40
An Education Worth Selling	Amanda Petefish-Schrag	43
Snowball	Luke Rolfes	46
Big Questions, Small Entanglements	Richard Sonnenmoser	48
I Regret Nothing	Elizabeth Stephan	59
The Loudmouth Begins	Alyssa Striplin	62
Beauty Inveterate	Helen Strotman	67
The Zoo	Clayton Stuart	72
Subjectivity, Objectivity and the Value of a University Education	Richard Toomey	75
Finishing the Book	Mara Wilson	80

Introduction

On March 22, 2013, the day before spring break, in a classroom in Colden Hall on the campus of Northwest Missouri State University, the students of English 512 Publication Skills made a decision. Over the previous week, the class had assembled a list of fifty possible titles. Some favorites had emerged, including "What Someone's Really Paying For," "College: Perseverance, Friendship, Self-Actualization, Balance," and "Love Letter to Binturong." We talked about how the book we'd imagined assembling in January was different from the book we'd actually made. We tried to articulate the "thematic threads" connecting, however tenuously, the essays to each other. We combined some of the titles on our list; we added some new ones. We heard arguments. We listened. Sometimes the room filled with that contemplative silence which years ago, when I began my college teaching career, would have made me break a cold sweat. Now, I relished the silence that meant people in the room were thinking deeply. Eventually the editors winnowed the list down to three, and then we voted.

Grit and Spit: The Dirty Truth of Academia, as a title, is the result of that day's class meeting. The book itself, of course, is the result of a more sustained effort. It's the result of hundreds of individual and group decisions made by the students of Publication Skills over the winter and early spring of 2013. *Grit and Spit* was edited—a process that included soliciting and then evaluating submissions, working with selected contributors on copyedits, typesetting the book, and choosing its cover art—by the nine students enrolled in Publication Skills. While the book was a class project for nine students at a particular university, and while it explores the experiences of students, faculty, and alumni at that same school, the editors hope that the book will resonate, and will explore questions about the value of the university experience, more broadly.

When the Publication Skills students began this project, I offered up a motivating question: What are places like

Northwest Missouri State University for? To attempt an answer, and to make this book, I knew my students would need to push beyond the statistics and clichés. They would need to get into the muck, to explore without sentimentality what was happening inside and outside of classrooms at universities like Northwest. They would need to ask our contributing authors to do the same.

According to sociologist Charles Tilly, when situations or events or emotional states are tough to explain—when they are "puzzling, unexpected, dramatic, problematic, or exemplary"—the most satisfying explanations tend to be stories.[i] There is much about university life that resides somewhere in the spaces between these adjectives: problematic and unexpected, puzzling and exemplary. I'm proud to have worked with a group of students who dedicated themselves to the unheralded and difficult work of getting other people's narratives into print, and I'm proud to introduce a book that includes so many stories that dramatize the problematic, unexpected, puzzling, and exemplary nature of learning, of maturing, of doing all the difficult, expensive, fascinating, and quotidian work of university education.

In "An Education Worth Selling," an essay advocating the value of liberal education, Amanda Petefish-Schrag argues that "imagination is the ultimate practical skill." She describes the value of what's often called "critical thinking"—the ability to "come at a problem backwards and upside down, inside out and sidewise"—and proffers some of the questions that universities should ask themselves and their students if they're serious about the development of the imagination. Another contributor from the teaching faculty, Richard Toomey, talks about how the meaning of scientific inquiry depends, in part, upon the imaginative capabilities that a liberal education is supposed to foster: "[I]n seeing how others express themselves through literature, the arts, philosophy, culture, mythology, and religion, we are able to gain perspective on what constitutes 'our' values."

According to Petefish-Schrag, one of the ways that liberal education has value is in preparing students to face the unexpected, to engender resiliency in the face of challenges. Many of the essays in this book discuss those challenges by describing personal and academic setbacks: Elizabeth Stephan's struggle to come back from academic suspension, Kate Dittmann's realization that her university friends were not exactly who she thought they were. Mara Wilson outlines about a dozen scenarios that made the choice to continue college difficult. Karlee Liberty and Chelsea Nichols explore balancing academic demands with social, financial, and familial responsibilities. Shea Boughton began a required field-experience class begrudgingly, but, through his not-always-pleasant experiences in Estes Park, Colorado, he learned some important lessons about people. Kori Binette calls the special combination of resiliency and self-awareness "grit," and her essay limns how powerful a determinant of academic success a little grit can be.

One "dirty truth" of academia might be that what's most valuable to outsiders—an employer, say—is primarily the credential, the degree in hand, but what's most valuable to the student about the college experience is usually something independent of the credential. This idea is demonstrated in Yahaya Gwamna's essay about his various leadership roles in campus organizations. Kara Huen hopes her future employers ask about her "unrelated activities," including the choirs she's been a part of at Northwest. The degree she's earning won't tell the people she meets everything about who she is and what she's passionate about. Likewise, the value of Samantha Compton's experience has been found not in the credentials themselves but in the transition from seeking one set of credentials to another. In that transition, she found her passion for theatre.

One curious, lovely element of this book is that its focus, especially among the student authors, is not the classroom. The book does not dwell, to relax into the cant of educators, on the methods of instruction or the delivery systems: the fifty-minute PowerPoint presentation, the meticulously designed lab experience, or even (to my chagrin) the seated-in-a-circle literary discussion. The most valuable part of the university experience—for authors such as Alyssa Striplin, Taylor Mothershead, Clayton Stuart, and Katie Hardisty—happens in those places where instructors are least visible. These authors are searching for meaningful human connection, for friendship; the university has value, in part, because it houses the living-learning environments of the fraternity house or the residence hall, or the working-learning environment of the campus writing center. Chief among the "gifts" Sarah Dittmann believes are bestowed upon college graduates is "a sense of who you are." After reading Alyssa Striplin's "The Loudmouth Begins," I understood anew how "self-actualization" might be a legitimate answer to the motivating question of this book.

In an earlier version of this introduction, I wrote that universities "provided a bridge between the hormonal fugue of adolescence and the anticlimactic responsibilities of adulthood." A few of the copyeditors in Publication Skills asked, rightly, whether readers might be confused by my locution. Luke Rolfes expresses the thought more elegantly. In "Snowball," Rolfes discusses the "fascinating limbo" of the traditionally aged college student: "freed from the nest" but still a "college kid" and "fledgling adult."

Helen Strotman's "Beauty Inveterate" braids many of these thematic threads. Strotman's exploration involves ideas about aesthetics and friendship, joy and suffering, family life and academics, naïveté and maturity. Her exploration of cynicism and its opposite involves the return of a family member's cancer and what a professor says during a class discussion. The beautiful, Stotman reminds us, exists in "a world where people fly planes into buildings" and where those we love die too soon, where suffering and joy are often unevenly heaped.

So, a picture's starting to emerge. The university that's represented in these pages is a social environment that enables learning from peers and mentors; it's an engine and purveyor and crafter of knowledge in its various forms; it's an incubator for creativity; it's something slightly more leisurely and enlivening than a vocational training center; it is still one of our culture's best providers of liberal education; it is where we struggle to grow up, where we learn to endure, where we discover anew who we are and who we might want to be.

We set out to explore what places like Northwest Missouri State University are for, what universities like ours accomplish, what value they provide. And to our motivating question this book provides a few partially formed answers. I say "partially formed" not to demean any of the contributors whose work the editors selected for publication. Rather, I believe the arguments and observations and stories in this book, if they're to have weight, if they're to bear the scrutiny of our readers, must necessarily be partial, provisional; they must be, like us, in progress.

—Richard Sonnenmoser
Maryville, Missouri
April 2013

Kori Binette
Instructor, English and Modern Languages

Time to Get Gritty: The Non-Academic Stuff that Makes You a Better Student

Ever since my first semester as a 23-year-old teaching assistant assigned to a classroom of composition students, my father has regularly asked me how many students I fail each semester. I don't indulge him in specifics, but there are, unfortunately, always at least a handful of students—sometimes more, sometimes less—who earn an F for the semester. It is, as every faculty member knows, one of the worst parts of this job. No one relishes thinking of the Fs on transcripts, of the teary conversations and fights between students and their parents that might follow, or of the disappointment and sadness students feel as a result.

What I want to tell my father, and what I want to share with each new batch of students, is that what I do when I assign grades at the end of the semester is only partially about any student's ability to learn material, apply concepts, or synthesize information. It's true that some students process information faster than others, and some come in with stronger preparation in English. Differences like these matter. But they do not matter to success as much as a student's grit. More and more, I'm convinced that this quality is what draws the line between success and failure in the university classroom.

But what is grit, exactly? In other contexts, we use it to describe the tough, hardscrabble neighborhoods of large cities or the available textures of sandpaper. In an academic context, grit tends to refer to the "habits of mind" that enable students to persevere in college. Researchers disagree about what exactly makes up grit: anything from "passion" and "self-discipline" to "curiosity" and "metacognition."[i] Sometimes, psychologists term these "non-cognitive factors." Nearly ten years into a teaching career, I see it as a kind of mental and emotional toughness. It's your mind's version of sandpaper: there to smooth down the edges for a cohesive finished product. Without it, everything remains raw material.

Grit can take a variety of forms in the college classroom, and I see it in all of my successful students. The student who comes to see me in my office at the beginning of the semester to discuss course expectations has grit. The student who, twenty-plus years away from high school, takes it upon himself to become computer literate has grit. The student who stays a few minutes after class on a Friday afternoon to ask a question about a paper has grit. The student who juggles raising children with full-time enrollment has grit. The student who raises his hand to ask the question everyone is thinking but no one else is asking has grit. It's a kind of stick-to-it-iveness, a not being afraid to look vulnerable or silly or even dumb. It's sometimes getting a low grade and not lashing out. It's tuning out what gets in the way of your goal. At its root, grit is confidence: the confidence of knowing that you are capable and worthy of the truly difficult work that is a university education.

A few scenarios may help to illustrate this idea:

- You study for what seems a reasonable amount of time for an exam. You are shocked when you receive a grade of 54 percent. How do you react to this disappointment?
- Your laptop crashes before you are able to submit an essay saved on it. The laptop is beyond resurrection. How do you handle this?
- You despise one of your instructors with a fiery passion, but this is the only instructor who teaches this required course. How do you make it through the semester?
- You've got a major presentation to give in class, and a half hour before class begins, your brother calls to ask you to pick him up from jail because he's gotten a DUI. What choice do you make?
- You're assigned to a group project and one member simply refuses to pull her weight. Your grade depends entirely on the group's work. How do you work with this peer to ensure everybody's success?

The pursuit of higher education presents students with many challenges, and not all of them are strictly intellectual in nature. There are no perfect "right" answers to those questions posed above, but there is such a thing as a pattern of grit. Grit determines how you react to difficult situations like these and therefore plays a large part in determining your success or failure. Grit does not mean that college is magically transformed into a carefree experience. Parts of it will still suck, and sometimes you will have to make a harder decision than you'd like. Sometimes you will have to be selfish in order to survive. You might have to overcome loneliness. You might have to miss your family. You might have to force yourself to feign interest in a subject to get through it. Grit will get you there.

Grit is not a panacea. There are real limits, and sometimes your life outside of school will mean that you can't continue. For example, maybe a family member is dying, maybe you're struggling with a chronic illness, or maybe you're going through a divorce. There are times when being in college is not the best thing for you because you have to be elsewhere for a while. Grit can't overcome life obstacles like these, but it can help you figure out when you need to walk away for a while.

Grit can get you back to where you need to be, too. A recent example: Three years ago, a student of mine withdrew from the class halfway through the semester. The student's written work was strong, and she had not missed any major assignments. The problem was that a significant family problem meant that she was doing a lot of traveling and caring for a relative. Though she was a good student, she decided to drop the course because she needed to concentrate on this other problem. Three years later, I am delighted to say the same student has returned to take the class again with me. Three years ago, she recognized that she was struggling, made the appropriate decision for her life, adjusted her course load for a while, and is on track to graduate in May. This is a story of grit.

In the end, a college education is more than the content of your major or your minor. In fact, that's generally of little importance, even to future employers. What matters is what the degree says about you: that you had what it takes. That you stuck with it. That you endured. That you smoothed out the edges.

Shea Boughton
Senior

A Class I Learned From

Here at Northwest Missouri State University, I have a minor in recreation. Students that have minors in recreation are required to do a course called "Field Experience in Recreation," and what that course entails is working somewhere in the field of recreation and logging your experience and telling the professor what you're experiencing as the class goes on. I was trying as hard as I could to find a place I could have this experience for the summer of 2012. Finding someone to let me work for them was a challenge in itself. I applied to many places such as Yellowstone National Park and Cedar Point Amusement Park. Unfortunately for me, I never received a response from them. My next attempt was trying to work in the Park and Recreation department of my hometown in Mount Pleasant, Iowa. I felt for sure I could get my class done there since I went to high school with the girl that was now in charge of the department. She informed me that she could not take me since she didn't have enough work for me to actually do. This was horrible news and I knew that I would have to try harder to fulfill this requirement.

I searched for jobs on the internet, and one job stood out as being something I could do and would fulfill this class requirement: working the front desk at a hotel in Estes Park, Colorado. I applied and within two days they interviewed me and I got the job. I couldn't believe that I was getting this job and I was able to avoid living with my parents for a summer. The idea of being surrounded by mountains every day seemed wonderful as well.

One of the things I learned from this class and my job is that hotel work is pretty stressful because of how mean people are. I got chewed out by mean guests every week. Sometimes this was my mistake; other times, I did nothing wrong.

One day, as I'm standing at my desk, daydreaming like I did every time at work, this married couple with their baby appeared at the front desk. I asked for their last name and instinctively I said out loud, "OK, it looks like I have found your room."

"I actually have two rooms."

"It . . . only says one right here."

"What? That is a bunch of bull! I called you guys yesterday and you guys said it wouldn't be a problem! I had two rooms with a crib for my baby!"

"OK, let me call the travel agency and see what happened to the other room."

"This is ridiculous! I called you guys yesterday and you said there was no problem and everything was fine!"

"Yeah? Well you didn't talk to me, so I am going to call and see what happened."

My manager rolled his eyes and laughed as I sat down on the computer and called Expedia as the father at the desk pouted about the situation. I started questioning why I even had this job.

"Hey, I'm at the hotel in Estes and I have this guy that says he has two reservations with you guys. I'm only counting one."

"Yes, he does have two reservations. It's just the second one is under his wife's name."

I walked out and said, "We found the reservation under your wife's name."

He burst out laughing and said, "Oh! I see, I guess it was just a big misunderstanding!"

I certainly didn't find it funny.

I feel like maybe there was a chance that getting yelled at was helping me grow as a person. That feeling I had was always challenged by the next group that would come along and yell at my co-workers and me.

One day I'm once again standing at my desk and it felt like a great day since the hotel was nearly booked and I was assuming that I wouldn't have to deal with anymore reservations for the day. In the middle of my shift a biker gang of about five came in to make a reservation. As nicely as I could, I smiled and said, "Nope, we are all booked for the night." They grimaced at me and walked away. It was only a couple minutes later when they came back into the lobby.

"We have a reservation now."

"No, you don't. We are all booked."

"We just went on Priceline. They booked us for two rooms."

I got on my computer to see what happened. We had recently blocked Priceline from making reservations in our system because they had been overbooking us recently. It turns out that an agent from Priceline went on Expedia and booked them rooms through their agency instead. I asked my co-worker Sindee what to do and she said, "We don't have the rooms. You're going to have to send them away."

I walked out of the office and said to the bikers, "I don't have the rooms. Expedia overbooked us and they made a mistake."

"We didn't book through Expedia. We booked through Priceline!"

"Yes, but, Priceline booked through Expedia. And they overbooked us, we don't have them."

"How could you guys not have rooms available, but their system says you do? How does that work? We should be able to talk to a manager!"

There was no manager on duty. It was the afternoon shift. It was really just me and my co-worker who also did not know how to deal with these bikers. The bikers just glared at me. I didn't really know how to deal with an intimidating stare down, so I awkwardly looked at the mean biker woman, rolled my eyes to the mean biker man, and just went back and forth. It was a weird moment, but I couldn't give in to their demands even if I wanted to. I was just going to have to put up with them until they gave up and left.

"I can write you a note, explaining what happened and you can give it to Priceline to get your money back."

The bikers let out a sigh and finally gave up. They took their note and decided to call Priceline to cancel and get their money back. The situation is funny to look back at now, but it wasn't funny at all at the time.

The experience I had wasn't completely full of mean people. Sure, there were other instances such as the guy who called me a douchebag because we were all booked for his particular night, or the woman who yelled at me because she "had to peel rat shit off her comforter." But there were other people I had met that I ended up becoming friends with to this day.

Living in the dorms behind the hotel I felt out of place with the people I was living with. A lot of the people I lived with were from foreign countries such as Ukraine, Russia, and Turkey. Going to work, or coming home from work, I would often see that they had made a disgusting mess in the living room. It seemed like the only hobbies they had were smoking and drinking all day. Their messes consisted of half-eaten sandwiches, empty beer cans all over the room, brownie crumbs covering the table, the trash can and recycling bin overflowing with garbage, as well as toys including a blue light saber and Barbie dolls they had placed in sexual positions. At one point I was like, "You know, I really just don't fit in this group."

I don't know what changed my mind, but one day I decided that I would try to hang out with them. It was weird considering the only times I had talked to them before was when they offered me a taste of Ukrainian vodka, as well as the week they were trying to get jobs at the hotel (and they yelled at me just like customers did). I sat down on the couch one night and watched the Olympics with them. The following day I decided to watch TV with them again, which caught the attention of their group.

Valeria, one of the girls from Ukraine, said, "I've never seen you like this before. This is the second day you have been social with us. Why are you doing this?"

"Well, Val," I began, "I thought I would just try hanging out with you guys for once."

There really wasn't a good explanation I could give her; I literally did just decide I would spend time with them. Soon we were going out to bars, the bowling alley, or even wrestling in the hallways. We would have theme parties where we would dress up like pirates and pretend our couches were boats. One week we had a Ukrainian-themed party, followed by an American-themed party the next week. Other times, commercials on TV for Mitt Romney and Barack Obama would appear, and I found myself explaining to my friends what those commercials actually meant and the views of each candidate.

I came to a realization that my beliefs about these people were completely wrong. I did fit in, and they welcomed me with open arms. Sure, I didn't know their culture, and I certainly didn't party as much as they did, but they never held that against me. They would even try to cheer me up after a bad day of work, and they would cut me off from alcohol if they felt I drank too much.

It felt like I had more of a purpose than just being in Colorado to do a job and complete a class; I now had a new opportunity to help international workers have a more enjoyable experience in the United States. Our reasons for being there may have been completely different, but our experiences soon came to be the same.

It is easy to reflect on the month of March 2012 and remember how much of a pain I thought it was to find a way to complete this class, but now I'm most certainly glad that it happened. The experience that my class gave me was an amazing one. I hope it was just as good for my friends from Eastern Europe.

Samantha Compton
Freshman

Acadakid Transitions

I remember my first few days at the Missouri Academy with great clarity. It felt like the summer camps I went to as a kid. There is always this feeling at camp, like you're wearing these rose-colored glasses and everyone gets along, like you have finally found this place where you fit in and belong. The Academy was like that.

I found people who had similar experiences as I did. There were a few students who were Duke TIPsters like myself, talented seventh graders who took the ACT or SAT for a Duke University study called the Talent Identification Program. A few of those students were even at the state recognition ceremony that caused me to ruin my perfect attendance and miss the last day of seventh grade.

I remember the deep philosophical or scientific conversations that would develop during lunch, like the scientific reasoning behind why the egg obviously had to come before the chicken. I think everyone enjoyed this because we would have just been ridiculed for trying to even begin a conversation about it in our sending schools. It was a kind of a rare, nerd heaven-on-earth. I didn't view myself as different until the traditional freshmen arrived.

Two weeks into my time at the Academy we were thrust into a real college world. Many incoming freshmen remember different events from Advantage Week, the week traditional freshman arrive on campus to get to know each other, and Academy students get to experience those too. I still have my color-changing cup from the ice cream social, and, though I never made it to the "Can I Kiss You?" program, I did get to see the comic from the week. But the activity that stands out most for me was the big meet-and-greet at

Centennial Gardens and all of the activities at the Bell Tower. I think this is because for the first time I realized what it meant to be an Academy student, since I had to leave early.

I remember getting advice from a community leader, the students who are supposed to be role models for first years and act a bit like non-disciplinary residential advisors, to just say I was a freshman, not mention I was only 16, and, if asked where I lived, to say North Complex or Douglas-Cooper but to avoid calling it the Academy at all costs. This was all to avoid being classified as "one of them." Frankly, I was terrified. This was an unnecessary feeling. I've found the Northwest campus to be a home for me. I've always felt accepted, which is one of the reasons I chose to stay here.

I found my second year at the Academy to be fulfilling socially, while lacking academically. To put it shortly, I hated physics. I hated science. Instead, I found myself drawn back to theatre and English, my first loves. I found ways to be involved as an Academy student. My first year I joined the forensics squad and made friends with a few theatre students. It was through them that I learned about ushering. I went to *Christmas Carol* earlier in the year and I wanted to go see *Our Town*, because I had heard a lot about it but had never actually seen it. The only problem was, I didn't have the money.

One of the girls on the squad told me about ushering as a way to see the shows. That was my first taste of the department: standing around, handing out programs and watching *Our Town*. I finished that year by also ushering for *See, Hear, Speak*, a collaborative show that Northwest students wrote with the help of Sean Christopher Lewis. Looking back, that was a major reason I decided to stay at Northwest. Our program isn't just *Our Town*, Shakespeare and Neil Simon; it's collaboration and innovation, creativity and originality.

I got even more involved my second year at the Academy. Let's face it, by this time, I *hated* math and science. I dreaded getting up in the morning to go to physics, and I dreaded doing my homework at night, so it wasn't that hard for me to realize that I shouldn't be in the math or science fields. Instead of focusing on academics, I started to focus on social activities and future endeavors. I quit the forensics squad to work on monologues for a scholarship audition, and I became the activities coordinator for Common Ground, the queer and ally alliance on campus. I ushered twice for *The Tempest* and saw it another three times. I went to black box shows, Comedy Inc. shows, and even a couple of showcases throughout the year. In February, I auditioned for the *Vagina Monologues* and got in.

This was my first time back on stage in any capacity since the summer-school show I did before my first year. I was so nervous, but there were theatre students in the show with me that I've come to call my good friends. They helped me through. Of course, all of this only made me more nervous for the upcoming year. I didn't want to be treated differently than any other incoming freshman and I was terrified that my classmates would hate me for knowing everyone already.

Of course, I was wrong. My first semester, as a traditional student, I was cast in the Freshman/Transfer show, *Wiley and the Hairy Man*, and I made friends. The friends I had made the year before became better friends and they've all gotten me through so much. Everything from being nervous for my *Midwives and Witches* audition to finals week of first semester. All of it was just a transition from the sixteen-year-old kid I was when I started in the Academy to the young adult I am now. I had to grow up a lot during my time at the Academy, but sometimes being a theatre major means I get to "grow down" just a little.

I love my life and my experiences because I wouldn't be who I am today without them. I joke around with my friends, saying that even if I end up living in a refrigerator box on the side of the highway, I can always go back to science, even though we all know that I won't. The education and friendships that I built in the Academy are what keep me going and strong today.

Kate Dittmann
Junior

My Wake-Up Call

The value of a university education is a topic so broad that I bet few people actually realize just how tremendously four years can or has affected them. Generally, without putting much thought into it, one could say that the value of a university education is that it prepares you for a better future, teaches you responsibility, and so on and so forth. I could talk about the educational aspect of going to college, but I honestly do not believe that the real, life changing value of the university experience comes from inside the classrooms or textbooks. I have been at Northwest for nearly three years now, and in that time I have learned more about myself and others than I had originally thought possible. That sounds cliché, but it is true. I've been severely depressed, felt small and insignificant, and overall just plain unhappy, but I've also been on top of the world, strong and powerful, and overwhelmingly content. I've been on both sides of the spectrum, and it's all because of the people I surrounded myself with.

In order to properly communicate what I'm talking about, I feel like it's only necessary to share the absolute worst and scariest moment of my life. But first, some quick backstory. My freshman year, I met a seemingly nice group of people, and they became my closest friends at Northwest. They introduced me to parties and alcohol, and I finally felt like I was one of the cool kids. These people were all from the same small town area and they had known each other for years. Even though I occasionally felt like I was the odd man out, it was nice to feel like I was part of a group most of the time. There was one specific, significant person in this group, and his name was Kyle. Kyle was funny, but in a way that was always at other people's expense. He was flirty, but he was always chasing after an ex-girlfriend back at home. He was smart but often thought about what was best for him instead of others. Regardless of these things, I fell extremely hard for him. We did a sort of "will they or won't they" dance for about a year, and then I finally gave up. I accepted that he never actually had any interest in being with me, just like how his ex-girlfriend never had any interest in getting back together. We were both just somebody else's fall back for entertainment.

Fast forward a month. Nothing had changed, and I had begun talking with another guy I had met in one of my classes. One night I brought him to the house where we all hung out to watch a basketball game, and I could immediately see the fury in Kyle's eyes. I had moved on to greener pastures. His stare was daggers. As the night progressed, Kyle got progressively more intoxicated. He tried to be friendly with me in ways I used to want, but I was not drinking and was not interested. I left and dropped my date (who by the end of the night I saw more as a brother, mind you) off at his apartment and made my way back to mine.

This is when my entire outlook on what I wanted in life changed forever.

My roommate had gotten a text from a mutual friend saying, "I'm warning you that Kyle is coming over. He's really drunk and he said he's going to break all of your and Kate's stuff." We immediately got scared, because we knew that Kyle was not a nice drunk (because he wasn't nice most of the time, anyways). We ran outside, locked our door, and were going to try to stop him on his way over. However, as we walked outside, we saw that he was already there. He walked right passed us in a blind fury, went upstairs, and attempted to open our door. Upon finding it locked, he began throwing his body full force into the door, trying to break it down. I screamed at him to stop, and he yelled a multitude of awful things back at me, including, "I'm going to hurt you, Kate. I don't care if it's physical, mental, or emotional. I'm going to hurt you." With this, he ran out the door.

We hoped that he was gone, and my roommate and I gathered ourselves before checking outside to see if the coast was clear. It wasn't. Outside, we found Kyle crouched down by my car, hubcaps thrown to the side, and there was a knife clasped in his hand. I am not a yeller. I am not a person who involves herself in bad situations, but here I was. Screaming at him, ordering him to give me the knife, I was in a situation that I thought would never happen to me. I ended up hoisting him up by the collar of his plaid shirt and pushing him away from my car. This is the only time in my life where I ever thought it was possible that a man might hit me.

Gesturing to the now-flat tires on my car, I yelled, "Do you even know what you are doing? You are breaking the law! Go home before I call the police!"

He stared at me. "I'm done with you, Kate," he said. "Don't ever talk to me again. Don't even try. I can't believe you showed up to the party with that guy—"

"What does *he* have to do with this?"

He stopped. I knew that question would end it all, because he would never be man enough to own up to the way he really felt about the situation. "Nothing," he said. "I'm done."

And he walked away, leaving any miniscule amount of friendship we had left behind him. My roommate and I returned to our apartment to find that our door had a massive crack down the side. If Kyle would have thrown his body into our door one more time, he would have broken in. This crack has served as a daily reminder of this lesson.

What is funny and incredibly sad about this situation is that Kyle was not alone. A mutual guy friend who was bigger and stronger than Kyle was with him, and he could have stopped the situation once he saw it progressing, but he didn't. As our mutual friends found out, they defended him with typical "it was because he was drunk" excuses. Zero of my friends offered comfort, and zero of my friends truly came to my aide. This whole experience made me realize that these friends that I had were not really my friends, because none of them seemed to care much about my safety or well-being. Thus far, this moment was the most alone I have ever felt in my entire life. I waited for an apology—from anyone—and it was never received. I spent the rest of the semester struggling through the days, crying more than I ever had, and leaving Maryville as soon as I possibly could.

As difficult as it was to return to Northwest after what I had been through, I knew I didn't really have a choice on the matter. I did, however, have a choice of what kind of people I surrounded myself with. I chose not to surround myself with people who excessively drank, who did not care about me, and were all around just a negative force in my life. I decided that I would rather be alone than unhappy. It did not take long for me to reconnect with old friends that cared about me, and to find a new place in the tiny town of Maryville where I knew I could be happy. I joined an organization, and I had a relationship with someone who treated me so well that I couldn't believe I ever put up with the way I had been treated in the past.

That right there is what I think the value of the university experience is all about. I had something awful happen to me, learned everything I could from it, and now I only allow myself to thrive. I learned not to settle, not to allow bad things to happen to me. I learned to change what was bad and replace it with good, and above all I learned to surround myself with what I knew I deserved. I may learn facts and theories in the classrooms at Northwest, but I learned about the value of my life outside the university walls. Don't get me wrong, there are some wonderful experiences that come with college, but this particular experience has majorly shaped what I expect out of life. I personally believe that it realigned my life. Before, my grades were good, but could be better. I was living for the weekend, even though sometimes I wouldn't remember it. I was settling for so many aspects of my life without even realizing it. With this behind me, I now go through each day looking towards the sky and focusing on the good, focusing on what I love, those who love me, and what makes me happy. I have even made the decision to change my major and to pursue a job that I am passionate about rather than one that will only pay the bills. I have learned to set myself up for happiness and success. The real value of my university experience was leaving the worst people I have ever met, so that I could recognize the best people I would ever meet when they walked into my life.

Sarah Dittmann
2004 Alumnus

How To Find Your Niche By Stepping Outside Your Comfort Zone

When I came to Northwest Missouri State University in 2001, I was confident in my ability to do well in school. However, I had yet to gain the confidence that I could succeed in the real world.

I stepped onto campus with little sense of who I was outside of other people. I often introduced myself in reference to others who had already established themselves on campus rather than relying on myself, my interests and my experiences to gain people's attention.

It wasn't until I got involved with campus publications, namely *The Northwest Missourian*, that I began to find out who I was and why I mattered, independent of anyone else.

Through my time at *The Missourian* and thanks to my Mass Communications professors, I developed my skills and became known as a stellar editor and solid writer. After putting in my time as a staff reporter, I was hired as the newspaper's copyeditor. I was a key part of an award-winning newspaper, and I was developing my own reputation—and gaining my sense of self along the way.

The beautiful thing about the Northwest experience is there are so many opportunities to explore your interests both in your major and outside of it. You can take a foreign language or a science elective even if you're an English major. You can take a newspaper or yearbook practicum even if you're a history major. You don't have to limit your sense of identity in any way while you're at Northwest.

What this allows you to do is find your niche. College is an incredible time for finding and shaping who you are in equal parts, and Northwest allows and encourages you to do both.

So what do you need to know as a freshman? Here are a few pointers.

Step outside your comfort zone. Living away from home for the first time is both exhilarating and daunting. Mom's not there to make you dinner after a bad day, and Dad's not there to give you a pep talk when you're feeling scared. But what you'll discover is that you have the strength and courage inside you to overcome the trials you'll face. It may mean changing majors, seeking out a counselor or trusted adviser to help you with a tough problem, or joining a new club with people you don't know. Northwest is a safe place to have these adventures.

Challenge yourself. My most rewarding class was also the absolute toughest one I took during my years at Northwest (Theories of Mass Communication with Fred Lamer, if you're curious). I've always been fairly good at the whole school thing, but that class made me work and hard. But you know what? I still use the information I learned in that class on a daily basis, whether consciously or otherwise. And more importantly, I learned that I was willing to work hard simply for the joy of learning rather than just to get a good grade.

Give yourself a break from time to time. College is supposed to be difficult. If you've done all you can do, and the choice is between getting a lower grade or pulling your sixth all-nighter in a week, then it's totally acceptable to let yourself end up with a B or a C. Adding another activity to your résumé when you're already overloaded and no longer enjoying the ones you're committed to is probably not worth it in the long run. College isn't just about getting the best GPA, earning the most honors, or developing the longest list of teams or organizations. It's about learning to live a balanced life, too.

The college experience is one I'm very thankful to have had at Northwest, but it's important to know that you will get out of it what you put into it. If you just go through the motions—show up to class but don't engage, attend hall meetings but skip other activities, do the bare minimum for your degree but nothing more—then you'll leave with a degree in your hand but not much else.

The good news is, at Northwest, there are so many opportunities to put in so much. You have excellent educators, a huge variety of groups and activities, and unlimited opportunities to explore who you are and who you want to be. What you give at Northwest, you get back in spades. When you leave campus as a student for the last time, degree in hand, you'll have a few of the greatest gifts of all: a sense of who you are and what you can achieve, the confidence it takes to succeed in the real world, and a team of Bearcats rooting you on.

Yahaya Gwamna
2012 Alumnus

The Value of a College Education

The value of a college education cannot be measured by statistics alone. What those statistics don't tell you are the other things that come packaged with the college experience. Some of your biggest life lessons are learned in college, through your many mistakes and triumphs. Undoubtedly you've had some. I know I have had mine. Whether it be getting that first or fourth MIP, spending a semester abroad, or finally getting an A on a test, they all act in synergy, molding the person you are today into the person you will be for the rest of your life. That weekend where you took things a bit too far and got charged with that MIP will give you a firsthand look at the dangers of alcohol abuse. That semester abroad increases your tolerance tenfold and you now have a whole new outlook on the world and the people that inhabit it. And the A on that test? That A has recommitted you to your studies, further convincing you and your parents that you're not just spending $20,000 a year to get your drink on.

The relationships made in school are worth the price of admission by themselves. You're meeting people from all walks of life who are completely different from you and yet quite the same. They're all trying to see what the big fuss is about, appeasing their parents, and looking for answers, answers you won't find or at least truly appreciate until you're gone. College gives you the opportunity to experience things that you wouldn't have the chance to out in the real world, things you need to experience before you can hit the ground running when you get there.

I was always involved in high school, but I took it another step further when I got to college, by associating myself with the multicultural organizations of Northwest. These organizations have minimal funding, so the only thing that keeps them running are the truly dedicated members and their faculty mentors. I joined MORE, Mentors Over Retention and Education, which was where I truly started to come out of my shell. I was introduced to cultures and backgrounds that I had only read about or seen on TV and came face-to-face with some truly humbling and life changing experiences, really seeing how the "other side" lives. I met people who were the first in their family to get to college, people from single parent homes, people who were accustomed to someone they knew getting murdered, and families who truly didn't know where their next meal was coming from. Through MORE, I became part of MMO, the Minority Men's Organization. I eventually became the president and with that title I began to appreciate the value of hard work. As the token black kid from a small rural town in Iowa, everything I was exposed to was like nothing I had ever experienced. I came to appreciate the things I did have and understand the point of view of others, instead of judging with no basis.

College is not for everyone, but I do believe it's for the majority of us. I'm a year out, and there's not one day where I don't wish I could be in a classroom, in a group meeting, or just out and about with friends. So for those of you who are on the fence or simply against going to school I truly urge you to reconsider because you won't experience anything like this. And don't get me wrong, I don't miss homework and I love working and becoming an independent member of society, but there was nothing like the four years that I had in college.

Katie Hardisty
Senior

Community Changing

As an out-of-state student, I've chosen to live on campus all four years. The floors I've lived on have all been great in their own ways. The trouble was with me. I liked the floors, but I never felt like I belonged. Part of the problem was that I have always been introverted, and it took tenacious people to get me to do anything besides hide away in my room. The rest of the problem was that I didn't feel like changing. I had supper once a week with a friend from high school and the friends that he introduced me to; to me, that seemed like all I needed in my social life.

Then, junior year, I made a friend of my own thanks to a creative writing class. She pointed out my lacking social abilities and insisted on helping me improve them. We got together for coffee and just talked about whatever came to our minds. Most of the time, we ended up laughing about how I would search Java City while trying to come up with a conversation topic when my turn to start a conversation came around.

She graduated, but the time I spent with her prepared me for the start of my senior year and the time I would spend on a new residence hall floor. It seems fitting to me that I started my university time in Franken Hall and I'm ending it in Franken Hall. The floor I'm on is community driven. Our RA encourages us to leave our doors open until quiet hours start and loves when we stop by the desk while she's on duty just to talk. My roommate is great; we had a while at the start of the year where neither of us knew what to do with the other, but our wacky personalities match. I've made friends with her friends that live next door to us. And, of course, I've made friends with others on the floor, too. Our floor tries to do fun things together whenever possible. Usually we have games of some kind on the weekends, and one night during the school week we have floor dinners where we all buy stuff for a meal and then someone that can cook throws it all together while the rest of us hang out in the kitchen and help however we can.

    I owe a lot to the friend that taught me how to interact with others again, but a lot of what's happened can also be contributed to finally finding the place where I can be me.

Kara Huen
Junior

Your Major is Not Your Only Place

When you went to SOAR, did you feel sort of lost and scared but, at the same time, really excited? Well, I was freaking out. I had a major and a plan all figured out, or so I thought. When we went to look at the schedules they had already created for us, I told them at the last second to change all of mine because I wanted to be a deciding major instead. I had too many passions, too many career paths, too many ideas of where I wanted to be in 4 years. What I wish someone had told me was not only is it not uncommon to be unsure, but more importantly that it is okay to be involved in more things than just what pertains to your major or your career.

As an English Education major, I surprise people in my hometown when they hear this. They all ask, "Why did you not go into music?" or don't even ask and just assume that I did. I've thought about it plenty, believe me. It took the longest time to finally figure out that my passions don't have to be given up no matter my career path. Even though this is my major, I am also involved in the Madraliers/Celebration Choir, Tower Choir, and Sigma Alpha Iota, a music business fraternity. I love to sing and it has always been a passion of mine. It's also wonderful to be part of a sisterhood that welcomes me, as well as a choir where everyone enjoys being there just as much as I do. Clearly these also have nothing to do with English or the education of it, but I knew I would not be as happy if I wasn't still a part of them.

Now, don't get me wrong. It is still worth it to take part in things that will also help you down the road on job applications. For instance, I work in the Writing Center and am a member of Sigma Tau Delta, the English honor society. The friendships I have made and the work that I have done are leading me in exactly the direction I want them to and they reassure me that I have chosen the right path to follow. I hope that future employers of mine look at these major-related things and ask what kinds of experience I have gained that I think will give me a leg up; I'll have plenty of answers for them. However, I hope they also ask about my unrelated activities, because I find them to be just as valuable.

What people too often tend to mistake is that if you aren't happy, it might not be what you're doing; it might be what you're missing. This was the case for me. English Education stuck out to me as a major because reading and writing is what I want to share with the world someday. It is something I could spend all day doing, just me and the paper. As much as I love music, I figured that this was something I didn't need to teach to be happy with. I just want to listen to CDs for a few hours, wear out my voice with the windows down in my car, or join a community choir in my free time. More importantly, though, are the books I want young adults to read, the essays I get to grade outside of work, and the constant study of English I will be doing every day. It holds more permanence to me, which helped me choose what to study and what to do for fun.

The point to all of this is that no matter what you decide you want to do with your life, you don't have to give up something else to be successful. You can love music, theatre, sports, history, English, etc. and find an organization on campus that you can join on top of your studies. Don't be afraid to put yourself out there and keep doing what you love. Find out where you can still be yourself and have fun on campus; I guarantee there's a place for you.

Karlee Liberty
Senior

A Week in the Life

"Headstrong" by Trapt is playing, and my phone is vibrating against the wooden bedside table. It's 8:00 in the morning. I have to turn it off quickly, so that it doesn't wake my fiancé. As soon as the sound stops, I roll over and go back to sleep. At 8:30, the alarm goes off again. This time it's "Famous Last Words" by My Chemical Romance. I turn it off, rub my eyes, drowsily get out of bed, blindly put on clothes, and don't do my hair or makeup. I kiss my fiancé, who is still sleeping, and go into the living room. I put on a coat, pick up the backpack that I made sure was packed the night before, and make sure to leave by 8:45. I walk to Colden, which, if I walk kind of fast, takes about fifteen minutes, because I have a small stride. I have my first class at 9:00. I sit down and the lectures blur together from 9:00 until 2:00. I stay in Colden Hall the whole time, hopping from classroom to classroom. After the final class, I walk home. I change for work, and sit down for an hour or so, and take a nap so that I can make it through work without being too drowsy. I go to work at the Union from 5:00 until close, which means I get off whenever my work is done, which is usually 8:30. I go home, and try to convince myself that it's worth doing homework, usually end up doing something for one of my six classes, and then going to bed.

This is my Monday, my Wednesday, and my Friday. On Tuesdays and Thursdays I don't have a set schedule; it varies. I work twenty hours a week while being enrolled in six classes that equal fifteen credits. I am a senior, graduating in May 2013. I am constantly debating with myself about what I need to do, because nothing seems to be worth it anymore. I hope I'm not alone.

There is an ideal balance for students: a balance between work and school, social time and work, and school and social time. These balances are hard to maintain though. My golden standard would be something like working between 15 and 20 hours a week so that the bills can get paid, make at least high Bs in my classes, be able to go out on Friday and Saturday night, be able to sleep at least eight hours a night, and manage an hour of working out each day. While this sounds like it may be feasible, it is actually a ridiculous amount of things to achieve, and it is really easy to get stressed out while trying. Personally, I have deleted the hour of exercising each day (though I manage to exercise once every 2 days or so), and my number of hours of sleep dwindles perilously low, and I scrape by with low B marks in my classes. It's just really hard to maintain a lot of items on your agenda when you're in college. Especially when the average class claims that you should be spending three hours studying for every hour you're in a lecture. That would mean that I would spend at least forty-five hours a week studying outside of class. This math is getting a bit sketchy. In a seven day week there are 168 hours. Ideally, I should spend fifteen in class, twenty at work, forty-five studying, and fifty-six sleeping. Now I am down to thirty-two remaining hours in the week. Divide that by seven days a week and I have four hours a day that I don't have anything to do. Take out two hours for eating meals and another for showering, getting dressed, and trying to convince myself to get out of bed and I'm down to one hour each day that I can just sit and veg out, except I'm supposed to work out an hour each day, so there goes that hour. A college student needs more free time than that, a lot more. Now, obviously, I don't study forty-five hours each week, and the time is spread unevenly through my week, but it's still an incredibly stressful workload to be placing on myself. It would be stressful for anyone! Students are all crumbling under the weight of the discrepancy of their idealized scheduling and the reality that that ideal is unachievable. And that is just how life goes; there really isn't anything that I can do about it.

Even though it is hard, and I don't always love what's going on, I have still spent four of the best years of my life here at Northwest. I wouldn't trade any of it for the world. I love that I'm here and that I'm learning and I'm getting experience. I love that I have friends who can help me out when I'm feeling stressed. Everyone goes through slumps where it's really hard to get back on your feet, but it's not the end of the world. It's communities like the one here at Northwest that can get you through it.

Taylor Mothershead
Junior

Finding Friends

My freshman year of college I came in knowing no one else save for my brother who was my roommate for the first semester. Going through high school I had never really had a large amount of friends. I preferred a small group who would hang out on the weekends or whenever we got off work. I wasn't much for going to parties or anything like that, so sitting in a buddies basement for marathon runs of *Dragon Ball Z* were pretty fun to me.

Upon coming to college however I left those few friends behind and was now forced to confront this new chapter of my life on my own. Probably one of the reasons I'm content with a small group of friends is that I'm not the most sociable guy in the world. I often refrain from speaking in groups of people I don't know unless I have something important to contribute. This makes finding new friends a bit difficult. I knew that I didn't want to be one of those guys that just shut themselves into their room after classes are done and doesn't really socialize with anyone. The social stigma against such people, and my own beliefs that such a lifestyle was not what I needed or wanted, spurred me to go to some of the meet-and-greet events the school held for freshmen to try and help them find new friends. Sadly I am not much of an "energetic" person either when it comes to social gatherings. I ended up just standing a bit awkwardly with some of the other less-than-enthusiastic students, and though we shared some sarcastic remarks between each other nothing really solidified any bonds of friendship between us, so I left about as successful as I had been coming in.

This didn't deter me much, though, as I knew that these kinds of things probably took time and classes hadn't even started yet. I eventually met up with some people I had met at SOAR the past summer, and we walked around campus a couple of nights and went to an ice cream social over by the park. Going in I thought I may have lucked out and found some people who had seemed pretty cool upon my first impression of them a couple months before. This perception however was quickly dashed to pieces as I actually started spending time with them. That's not to say that they weren't good people. They weren't doing anything illegal like stealing cars or kicking small puppies. The problem I had with them was that they were too immature.

We were walking around campus one night and being new we soon found ourselves a bit lost, a concept that perplexes me now that I am familiar with the place. They were very animated and excitable in trying to find our way to some function or another, and when I advised we use a map, which I had carried with me at the time, they quickly waved the idea away saying that they wanted "an adventure." This small, almost inconsequential exchange quickly soured any potential interactions I could have with these people. Now I'm all for a bit of fun. My best friend back home and I often acted as foils to each other's personalities; he was the crazily excitable guy and I was the more level headed one. Despite his more eccentric tendencies, however, he also exuded a healthy amount of common sense, something I failed to perceive from the people around me that night.

So I continued my search. I went to a few more events on campus. I even attended a few club meetings that seemed like they might be fun and catered to some of my interests. A couple of these turned out to be a bit too hardcore for my tastes; there was one where they actually came out and said during a meeting that a lot of the people in the club had problems with having to drop out of classes and college all together due to focusing too much on playing videogames. As a self-proclaimed casual gamer myself, but with an intention to graduate from the university, I realized this group wasn't for me. A writer's club looked promising as well, but after hearing one member mention their Transformers slash fiction and the lack of any officially sanctioned meeting place causing sporadic dates, I stopped participating in that club as well.

The high-rise I lived in didn't yield any more promising results. The floor I lived on and the building in general was chocked full of, my brother excluded, rowdy alcoholics who would blatantly ignore quiet hours and had developed a most annoying habit of pulling the fire alarm during the middle of the night. I had once attempted to step outside my room to go get dinner from the station, only to stumble upon my neighbors in the middle of a game of shoe bowling using the hallway as the lane. With no real direction in which to get out I decided to stay in and see if I couldn't find a cup of ramen noodles lying around somewhere.

I soon became frustrated and a bit panicked as all my attempts to find even one like-minded person were failing me one after the other. I began to wonder if I had done something wrong. I had followed all the "sage" advice people always spouted about how in order to make friends you needed to get out there and meet new people, and none of it had worked! It was now past midterms and I still hadn't found even a single person to call a friend. My brother had, as usual, had much better luck than me on the subject and had found a few friends from another dorm that he would hang out with on a regular basis. After tagging along with him after classes one day I found out that I knew a couple of these people from my classes and had even held conversations with them during class. I began to join my brother, spending our time after class and during the weekends over at the other dorm that our friends lived in and soon found myself part of a group. I had finally found people to socially interact with and found myself having a great time.

When the next semester came around my brother and I both transferred to their dorm and even managed to have our entire group live on the same floor. Not only was it so much easier than commuting there from my last dorm, but the floor in general was so much more different than my previous one. There was a far greater sense of "community." People would actually walk around past your door, or if they saw you in the study lounge they would smile and say hi. Looking back it was surprising how quickly things changed. I began to have so much fun that I soon forgot all the stress and anxiety I had been feeling just months beforehand about being alone and not being capable of finding friends, and it almost felt like another lifetime. Having people to spend some downtime with and de-stress from a hard school week isn't something to take for granted, and can help you in numerous ways.

Sometimes when I'm at other dorms I'll see a person who has shut themselves in their room without really socializing with the rest of their floor, and I feel relieved that I'm not one of them. I know just how damn lucky I am to have found friends and just how easily I could have ended up as one of the many self-shut-in students. I am immensely grateful that I was able to find the friends I have today and to have kept the ones from my hometown. Friends aren't something I've learned to take lightly, and I intend to try and keep in touch with them as the college years end, as best I can. So if I had to give someone advice on the matter I would tell them that it may take a long time to find friends in a new place, a lot longer than you may like, but when it does happen you'll find that it's usually well worth the wait.

Chelsea Nichols
Senior

The Art of Juggling

I'm twenty-one years old and a future English educator of high school and middle school. I am getting married and graduating in three and a half years from a program that usually takes four and a half. All of these things are a part of my life in college. I live a hectic life trying to juggle everything I have to do. I'm trying to make time for school, friends, traveling two and a half hours home, and frantically planning my rapidly approaching wedding with a fiancé, who also lives two and a half hours away. Needless to say, my whole life needs to be carefully scheduled just to have time for it all, and I feel it necessary to compartmentalize my life just to keep myself sane. One of the hardest parts of going away for school was leaving behind everyone. I have had to learn how to deal with being away from all of my loved ones and being in a place where I didn't know anybody. Although these last three and a half years have been tough, I wouldn't change anything.

My life at Northwest began before I even got here. I had to decide whether I was willing to move two and a half hours away from my family and my boyfriend for school. When I came to visit, I was drawn by the beautiful campus and the way that I was treated like a person, instead of as a number. I visited a couple other colleges around my home in Nebraska, but they were too big and didn't have the homey feel that Northwest had. Even though it was a two-and-a-half hour drive, I was coming to Northwest.

Throughout the last three years, there have been many moments filled with gut-wrenching homesickness. The worst part of being so far away was knowing that I left six younger siblings at home. Right before I left, my younger sister finally decided that she really liked me. My freshman year she would call me and ask me when I was going to come home. These conversations with her almost always left me in tears. I had to try to figure out how to spend time with my family without spending all of my money and time driving home. Now that she is a little bit older, my sister is busier with her own life in the first grade, but she will still call me every so often and make me feel that strong desire to be home with her.

I go home about once every month, but I don't get to see all of my family, because they live in two different places. When I left, I realized that there was a good chance that my youngest sibling, who was two, wouldn't really know who I was when I finally came home. My brother remembers who I am, because I spent enough time with him when I could. My family also spent a lot of time showing them pictures of me and talking about who I am. Unfortunately, I missed another huge milestone in my family's life. My dad and stepmom were going to have another baby. My second semester at Northwest I missed the first couple of months of my brother's life, because I was busy at school. Now, he is two years old, and he is still unsure of who I am and how I fit into his family. While that breaks my heart, I realize that at some point I can make it up to him by spending time with him as he gets older. There are plenty of years ahead for my siblings, but to accomplish my dreams, I need to be in college right now.

College has been a tough experience for me. I've been challenged in more ways than I would have thought possible. Isn't that the point of college, though? College is supposed to force you to break through your boundaries. You are asked to do things that you've never been asked to do before. It is a very intimidating journey, but it is also freeing. During these last three years, I have come to better understand who I am and what I believe in. I have experienced a lot during a short amount of time, both academically and personally. Now that I am almost completely through it, I can see how these experiences will be present throughout the rest of my life. I've learned how to have it all with what I want and what I need if I work hard and prioritize what is most important in that moment. College has shown me my strength to persevere. It has been tough, but so is life—and I'm ready for it.

Amanda Petefish-Schrag
Associate Professor, Fine and Performing Arts

An Education Worth Selling

One of my favorite plays is *On the Verge* by Eric Overmyer.[i] The play is about three Victorian women explorers who inadvertently discover time travel in their search for Terra Incognita—the last unexplored reaches of the world. Besides the generally quirky plot, I love the play because it deals with the liberal arts; it explores the intersection of language, geography, history, science, anthropology, and art. In incorporating all these disciplines it becomes a play fundamentally about the imagination, about the creative act and the ability to invent a world that transcends the sum of the parts we inherit. This idea of imagination innately connects to the purpose of the university degree.

Now when I speak in terms of imagination or creativity, I'm not using the terms in the way our contemporary culture would define and limit them. This isn't about wearing scarves and interpretive dancing our way to world peace and economic security, and I am not confining the teaching of imagination to those of us "artsy fartsy" types. We routinely separate the terms *arts* and *sciences*, yet both the physicist and the painter must be equally imaginative to practice their craft. Whether we call it creativity, or critical thinking, or problem solving, or innovation, the purpose of the university is to teach students to come at a problem backwards and upside down, inside out and sidewise. In short, the purpose of the university degree is to train the imagination.

Today, part of this training involves rescuing the imagination from the abuse and neglect it has suffered at the hands of contemporary culture. Part of what studies such as *Academically Adrift* reveal is that there is a disjoint between what students have been taught prior to entering the university and what the world requires from them upon leaving it, a disjoint that the university must address.[ii] K-12 education may use a "drill-it-and-kill-it," "teach-to-the-test" approach to education, but that doesn't mean that the "real world" mimics a standardized test. Students may have been taught to demand "right" answers and "easy" access to information, but a Google search will never provide a solution to global food shortages nor will it help them navigate their way through their jobs, their marriages, or any of the other complicated issues and relationships that will define their lives.

We need look no further than reality television or any number of twenty-four-hour news hosts to witness the assault on imagination that students face within our culture. Perhaps we should consider a university degree a sort of inoculation against *Jersey Shore,* or at least what it represents.

During the first week of the semester, my Theatre Appreciation students examine a popular entertainment as though they were anthropologists attempting to understand our contemporary culture. Reality television is usually their entertainment of choice, and their observations are telling. I'll share a few:

"We yell a lot."

"We drink too much."

"We don't listen to each other."

"We care more about appearance than being smart."

"We aren't very ambitious about anything important."

"People will do anything for money."

"We only see things one way."

"Kindness is weakness."

And one of my personal favorites, "Punching someone is easier than changing."

If a university degree is to be an inoculation against these ideas, it must also provide an alternative. Our universities need to provide the call to arms for living creatively and imaginatively. They need to provide a sort of imagination boot camp. Salman Rushdie says that the role of the artist is "to name the unnamable, to point to frauds, to take sides, start arguments, shape the world, and stop it from going to sleep."[iii] A university education allows students to play that role. The ability to see through multiple perspectives, to provide context, to see opportunity in challenge, is the value a liberal arts education is designed to provide. But that also requires that the university community embrace what the culture at large might have us abandon: interdisciplinary and humanistic approaches to the subject matter within and outside of our own curriculum, academic rigor, active engagement with students and the material in a variety of contexts. Imagine what a university degree would look like if we fully abandoned the notion that the liberal arts—that advanced training in higher-level thinking—are reserved for the academically and economically elite? If we advocated that education from multiple perspectives and contexts may matter most to those students who do not rank in the top 10% of their high school graduating classes? What would happen if we stopped advising students to get their general education courses "out of the way" and instead encouraged them to use general education to develop their point of view, their ethics, their mental aptitude? What if we collectively rejected the tendency to view general education as the rent we pay to keep our majors? If we taught and structured it as if it really mattered?

My guess is that such a university degree would be difficult to market to well-intentioned parents who want guarantees of specific employment and monetary rewards, or to politicians who want objective data that verifies student success, even if that definition of success is painfully limited in its scope. But perhaps that's part of the obligation we bear as the holders of university degrees—reframing the debate on the value of education.

Maybe we start by being honest in what we sell to students and parents. Maybe we start by saying obtaining a university degree is difficult because it has to be in order to prepare you for a lifetime of learning. Imagination takes work. And time. And discipline. It requires you to think beyond the obvious, and rise above the status quo. But here's the reward: Imagination is the ultimate practical skill. As the world changes, you won't be caught unaware. You will change to meet the needs of the day. You will see opportunity where others see dead ends. You will be equipped to look within and without, to discover your ability to empathize, to see consequences beyond the obvious, to live ethically under difficult and confusing circumstances. In short, when your profession changes, when your family changes, when your city, state, world changes, as they inevitably will, you will have better choices than punching someone.

The epigraph to *On the Verge* is a quote from André Breton: "Perhaps the imagination is on the verge of recovering its rights." I like to imagine that that is true. And I also imagine that a university degree helps get us there. That's a truly noble purpose, and it's one worth selling.

Luke Rolfes
Instructor, English and Modern Languages

Snowball

When I look outside the window of Colden Hall, I see a giant snowball. This snowball is over seven feet high, twenty-one feet in circumference, and it was rolled into existence by several of my students. The ball of snow is a world-record-breaking ball of snow, my students tell me. They've measured it with scientific instruments. They've contacted *Guinness World Records*. The only worry, of course, is that *Guinness* didn't send an official representative to oversee and record the snowball's construction. The record keepers, without physical evidence of creation, might question the legitimacy of the ball. This gives my students a reason to worry, especially because their snowball came to be as an organic expression of community. Mega-Snowball defines their university experience. It gives their time on campus an identity, and *Guinness* could potentially ruin that. But to me and the rest of my twenty-five students peering out the frosted windows of Colden Hall, there is no question. This is the biggest snowball in the world.

The snowball brings up one of the most interesting things about college students and one of the reasons why I get such a kick out of being around them. They are, more or less, trapped in a fascinating limbo. On the one hand, they've been freed from the nest. Their parents are not looking over their shoulders telling them when to go to class or how much attention to pay in class. Nobody is there to judge them if they eat pizza for breakfast, go moonlight sledding on cafeteria trays, or spend an entire evening arguing about the social implications of *Jersey Shore*. They are, for the first time in their lives, free to do as they please, and they wear these freedoms proudly, like badges on their sleeves.

Despite their newfound independence, students struggle to recognize themselves as being grown up. They are college "kids," fledgling adults, too old to be sheltered but not quite ready for the real world. They want to be identified as men and women, but they appreciate their youth in a way they never did in high school. Maybe the undefinable nature of their age leads them to construct a giant ball of snow outside Colden Hall. They need to figure out what kind of people they will become, and they need to let their childhood breathe at the same time. They want nostalgia; they want responsibility; they want respect. But they hold the right to be ridiculous if the spirit of the moment allows.

As my class beholds Mega-Snowball in all its glory, we remind ourselves how a perfect storm of expectations creates the vibrant and unpredictable landscape in which we all live. It was like the day I stepped outside the student union to find the passersby no longer hypnotized by their iPhones but instead looking up to a sky full of tens of thousands of migrating snow geese. My students never stop surprising me. We're all a part of this landscape, they tell me. We're just trying to figure out what that means.

Richard Sonnenmoser
Assistant Professor, English and Modern Languages

Big Questions, Small Entanglements

> Perhaps the most daunting challenge facing those of us who believe in the universal value of liberal education is the challenge of conveying its value to anyone—policymakers, public officials, and even many academics—who has not personally experienced it.
>
> —Andrew Delbanco, *College: What It Was, Is, and Should Be*

The cherry trees outside my apartment were blossoming, but the odor was sickly pungent: perfume sprayed onto warm garbage. It was spring 2000. The weather was beautiful—sunshine, evocative breezes—but the air in Columbia, Missouri, where I was in my second year as a student at the university, seemed strangely thin. I was behaving in ways I couldn't explain: skipping classes that I liked, sleeping during the day and staying up all night, making noises to my friends and parents about transferring to a college in my hometown while simultaneously applying for volunteer work and internships in Columbia. Maybe I could go full-time at the bar where, twice a week, I washed dishes and took money at the door. Maybe I could move to Lawrence, Kansas, where I had friends in indie-rock bands on national tours. Nothing felt right. And I wondered whether the problem might be what I did with most of my time: attending and preparing for classes at the university. Couldn't I still do what I enjoyed in my life as a student—reading, writing, thinking—outside the confines of the university? And wasn't continuing college evidence that I'd given up on my dream, which I'd convinced myself was being in an indie-rock band on a national tour? I started to fantasize—about quitting.

I limped to the finish line that semester, and in June I went to Ireland. For a week my traveling companion, a friend from high school, and I camped on the western coast, near Galway.

One night a bartender asked us if we were planning on looking for work, maybe extending our stay for a summer or a year. "Nights, work in a pub," he said. "Days, work on your novel."

"Well, I hadn't thought of *that*," I said.

My friend and I decided to separate during the days, so I had a lot of time to write. On buses and park benches and in our tent pitched on the shore, I wrote some deeply embarrassing poems in what I thought was the style of Seamus Heaney. My prose resembled too closely my favorite scene from James Joyce's *A Portrait of the Artist as a Young Man*. In my journal I tried to write my way through what I should do when I returned home. (I hadn't ruled out working in Ireland, but I decided that, if I chose that option, I'd rather do it legally and without sacrificing my roundtrip ticket.) I struggled through the decision of whether or not to return to the university.

I've been in one university or another ever since.[i] So, how did I get from thinking seriously about giving up to, well, making a series of choices that resulted in me never leaving?

What brought me out of my sophomore slump is a complex story involving, as I see it, both big ideas and small entanglements. To explore big ideas, that's one possibility for what undergraduate education at universities is for: the give-and-take, the debate, the artistic creation, the historicizing, the dramatizing, the inquiry, the experimenting, all those processes that involve people posing big questions and then searching with each other after answers; the small entanglements are what helped me stick it out long enough to realize as much.

"College," I used to say in a presentation for high-school juniors and their parents, "is expensive, difficult, and optional." This line was part of the script for the College Planning Workshop, a presentation that admissions officers at the University of Missouri gave as part of the school's public-service mission.

When I said that college is expensive, heads would nod. My audiences understood the finances of college attendance implicitly. Recent data from the National Center for Education Statistics indicates that the total cost for attending a public, four-year institution is, on average, over $20,000 per year. Private colleges and universities typically cost more. Depending on the type of institution, 70 to 90 percent of students receive some form of financial aid.[ii]

49

When I explained my use of the word *optional*, a member of the audience would usually interrupt me to say, "Not for my kid!" or "Not in this economy!" College attendance is as highly encouraged by our culture as it is discouraged by the prohibitive pricing; many students may not feel that stepping into their first college classroom is a free exercise of choice. They may not have the sense that they are choosing college from a menu of equally viable alternatives. Still, college remains, officially, an option. You don't have to go. Once you've enrolled, you don't have to stay. And the choices keep coming: where to attend, what to study, how to pay for it.

Difficulty is certainly subjective, and it would be inaccurate to claim that every course of study at every college is difficult. Some recent scholarship—notably Richard Arum and Josipa Roksa's *Academically Adrift* (2010), which concludes that students may be learning less and studying less than previously thought—has caused many to question whether the college experience in the United States is rigorous enough. Difficulty, though, may not only be intellectual, the mind-stretching work of doing calculus for the first time, or of reading Jacques Lacan or Donna Haraway or, for that matter, Virginia Woolf or William Shakespeare. Some of the challenges involve attitude, perception. The most trying conversations I've had with undergraduates at Northwest Missouri State University were not about hard-to-understand literary theorists or knotty concepts related to writing fiction. They were about the consequences of plagiarism or months-long absences, the unique limbo of family medical crises, or how college just doesn't seem "right" for the student. Even if the conclusions of *Academically Adrift* are correct, many students are nevertheless finding parts of the college experience difficult.

Difficult, expensive and optional—and, of course, students don't have the luxury of alternating between these states, at their leisure. The difficult, expensive, optional college experience is happening all at once and all the time. The day the tuition check is due is also the day of the exam on Rococo painters. The five-page essay draft must be submitted the morning the decision must be made about whether or not to take off for the coast—and for most of us, I think, some version of this choice happens every day.

During my second semester as an undergraduate at the University of Missouri, I took a humanities course with a professor in the English department, Howard Fulweiler, who had a white beard and lived in a beautiful Queen Anne home, where he once hosted my class for a semi-formal dinner. He was, late in life, learning to play the piano. He once asked me why, before coming to college, I hadn't read Samuel Taylor Coleridge's *The Rime of the Ancient Mariner*, and he seemed unable to comprehend, in a way that was somehow both humorous and deeply intimidating, my answer that it had never been assigned to me. Sometimes he wore a bow tie. For all of these reasons he was, to my mind, the university professor *par excellence*.

Once, in the minutes before a class discussion about Miguel de Cervantes's *Don Quixote*, in English translation, a student seated near me got exercised about the university's modern language requirements. She held her mouth in the way of a child who's been given some confounding news about her birthday party; she was nineteen, but she'd worked herself to the edge of a tantrum. She protested that she didn't need to know a language other than English for her desired career. She wondered if Professor Fulweiler, who often claimed he was the most tenured professor at the university, might be able to sign a slip that would allow her to not have to take these language courses. Maybe he could convince whoever needed convincing that the rules should be relaxed for her. After a few minutes of patiently nodding and smiling at this student, Professor Fulweiler calmly said, "Well, all that makes a certain kind of sense, I suppose. But wouldn't you rather be smart than stupid?"

I think of Professor Fulweiler and the angry student as stand-ins, or embodiments, for two competing ideas about what a college education should be about.

On one side of the spectrum—with Professor Fulweiler—is liberal education. If you are taking a wide variety of courses in a wide variety of subjects, if your college or university emphasizes diversity of educational experience, if your academic life does not seem to be leading to one particular "educational outcome," one particular job, you might be receiving a liberal education. The emphasis in such a system is usually on developing habits of mind rather than on learning particular skills for a particular job. The student receiving a liberal education is expected to interact meaningfully with what nineteenth-century literary critic and poet Matthew Arnold called "the best which has been thought and said in the world."[iii] In various forms, sometimes as the only course of study and sometimes as part of a university's general education program, this kind of teaching and learning is happening, though maybe not as much as its advocates would like, at colleges and universities in the United States and abroad.

Liberal education is an idea rooted in the concept of liberal arts, or *artes liberales*, what non-slaves in paternalistic ancient Greek society might pursue, to their betterment, in pursuit of the good life, in their leisure. Lately I've been toying with the idea that Northwest Missouri State University might rename its liberal arts curricula, which in conversation with members of the community is usually saddled with the bland word *general* and the equally unsexy *requirements*, Core Curriculum for Free Men and Women.

On the other end of the spectrum from liberal education might be the vocational models of for-profit universities. A recent television advertisement pitches Strayer University's "personal education plan," which is structured around credit awarded for what I would call non-university, or perhaps extra-university, activities: raising children, rebuilding an old car, or starting a business.[iv] If a liberal education is about sustained academic inquiry into culture, into the best of what's been thought and said, then the goal of a more purely vocational model might be the credential, the college degree. In such a model, keeping the customer satisfied is worried over as much as academic rigor.

In an episode of PBS's *Frontline*, "College Inc.," Mark DeFusco, a former president of Phoenix University, answered journalist Martin Smith's question—"Is education a business?"—by saying:

> I believe so. Listen, I'm happy that there are places in the world where people sit down and think. We need that. But that's very expensive, and not everybody can do that. And so for the vast majority of folks, who don't get that privilege, then I think it's a business.[v]

If the university is a business, then perhaps I should have said that customer satisfaction is worried over more than academic rigor.

I've presented the university in black and white, as either vocational credentialing service or provider of liberal education. Liberal education and vocational models are certainly in competion, but they are not mutually exclusive. Matthew Arnold's ideal may be happening at some universities. Mark DeFusco's may be happening at others. But what's happening at most universities is probably a combination, something in grayscale.

At most colleges and universities, even the remaining liberal-arts colleges in the U.S., there is at least some vocational training going on, or at the very least an acknowledgement that free men and women might eventually need to become gainfully employed free men and women. And, despite what Mark DeFusco says, I'm as yet unconvinced that those students who profess to want purely vocational training—"the vast majority of folks"—might not also be interested in or in need of investigations into ideas, the encouragement of academic experiences that, as Matthew Arnold said, "[turn] a stream of fresh and free thought upon our stock notions and habits." Just because the Strayer University advertisement promulgates the reductive view of universities as primarily credentialing services, as places to queue up for a degree, that doesn't mean that the desire for a liberal education has died, that college students everywhere might not hunger for the economic benefits of a college degree *and* something else.

That "something else" can be scary. The student receiving a liberal education must, deep down, acknowledge that there might be something wrong, or at least in need of re-evaluation, with his or her "stock notions and habits." Professor Fulweiler wanted me to read *The Rime of the Ancient Mariner* because he thought I might like it but also because he thought that it might help me to see the world anew. He wanted to rattle my cage intellectually; he wanted to goad me into asking more significant questions about beauty and truth.

Andrew Delbanco is correct; explaining the value of a liberal education to those who haven't experienced it is difficult.[vi] I'd add that it can be equally difficult to explain the value of a liberal education to someone *in its midst.* Simply enrolling in a first-year composition course or a survey of American history does not by default result in a conversion experience. No matter how much politicians and policymakers and university administrators might wish it to be otherwise, the value of a liberal education is likely to be deeply personal, difficult to quantify, and perhaps, more often than not, ineffable.

I wish I could say that, on a strangely cold June night near Galway, having come back from visiting the musty, cramped childhood home of Nora Barnacle, the wife of James Joyce, and that, sleepless, I emerged from the tent and saw, on the pebbled shore, and against the backdrop of the dappled sky, a lone white horse—and somehow the sight of that horse, and the beauty of the Irish coast, let me know that I needed to devote my life to universities and the ideas that they create and share. (My traveling companion, who was also ambivalent about returning to college and who now teaches middle school, did see such a horse, and against such a sky, but neither his lovely description nor my visit to Nora Barnacle's childhood home helped me to reach any conclusions.) I wish the story of what brought me out of my sophomore slump involved a Joycean epiphany, but it doesn't.

In the summer of 2000, and still thinking about quitting college, I began an internship with a literary magazine, *The Missouri Review*, where I read fiction and poetry manuscripts and eventually assisted in editing special features. That fall I reduced my hours at my bar job and began volunteering at a place called the Rainbow House, a shelter for children. Over the next few months, I became better friends with some of the other creative writers at the university, went to some parties, became a part-time houseparent at the Rainbow House, wrote some stories and poems that weren't emulations of Irish writers, started to study beside (not *with*, since we didn't share any classes) a pre-med friend from the residence hall, talked to my professors during their office hours, became a regular at "'80s Night" at a bar called Shattered, talked to my professors about pursuing graduate school, fell in love with Vladimir Nabokov's *Lolita*, went to see John Updike read at the student union, fell in love with Lorrie Moore's "You're Ugly, Too" and Amy Hempel's "In the Cemetery where Al Jolson is Buried," watched *Dawson's Creek* with my roommate, fell in love with Vladimir Nabokov's *Pale Fire*, watched *Sex and the City* with my roommate's sister, went to see my friends' band, The Appleseed Cast, play at a local club, talked to one of my professors while walking from Tate Hall to the parking garage, went to see Adrienne Rich read at the student union, played some original songs for a small crowd gathered at the Music Café, went on a research trip with the editors from *The Missouri Review* . . . .

No epiphanies—just small entanglements.

At the time of my sophomore slump, I was nursing a delusion. I believed I could enact my indie-rock or working-in-an-Irish-pub fantasy while simultaneously reading and writing and growing intellectually. I'd convinced myself that college wasn't helping me think. I thought that I could, on my own, without all the expense and difficulty of class schedules and grades and requirements and the expectations of my professors, get a liberal education. I thought, in a free society where I had access to books, journals, and the internet, I didn't need the university to do intellectual work, to ask big questions.

Of course, college isn't the only way to read books, think big thoughts, investigate questions scientifically or artistically, and inquire into whatever ideas seem worthy of exploration. But I wasn't seeing something else—something important—clearly.

In the months after returning from Ireland, I took a course in literary criticism in which I was assigned Vladimir Nabokov's *Lolita* as well as some critical essays responding to the novel. My mother said she hated "even the idea" of Nabokov's novel and wouldn't read it. Most of the students in my Literary Criticism class seemed to think that Humbert Humbert, the self-confessed pederast and murderer who narrates the novel, was really charming. Did I agree? And, if I did, what did that say about me? After finishing reading the novel, I called my mother and told her that I loved the book. When I got off the phone, I realized that I wasn't sure why I loved it. Was it the language, the nuanced playfulness of the prose? All the silly anagrams and cerebral games? What about the characters? Did I sympathize with Dolores Haze? Was I convinced by Humbert's confessions and lamentations? Did I like the idea that this was a "road trip" novel very different from *On the Road*, which had left me feeling antsy and underwhelmed? What did my reading of Nabokov's novel have to do with what I was learning in my other classes—Social Deviance, Human Sexuality, Psychological Anthropology—about pedophilia, the social construction of even "objective" science such as medical knowledge and practice, the existence of so-called culture-bound mental illnesses?

With *Lolita* as a text, and in the context of a class where we'd also read Thomas Hardy's *Tess of the d'Urbervilles* and Mary Shelley's *Frankenstein*, I was made to ponder questions about beauty and truth and justice. I thought about these questions in class discussions with Dr. David Read and the twelve other students in Literary Criticism. I thought about them, alone, while writing my assigned essays. I had a developing thesis, prompted in part by some of the assigned cultural criticism, about *Lolita* as an artistic rumination on exile; the novel explored, I thought, the similarities of being exiled from one's country and being exiled from one's childhood, that is, growing up. I thought about my thesis anew when Dr. Read handed back my final essay, with comments. I thought about it again when I asked Dr. Read to be my senior thesis advisor; I wanted to pursue the idea about exile a little further. I thought about a whole new set of ideas when I prepared for and took the Literary Criticism final exam. I thought about big ideas, in short, when I was asked to sit down and think about them.[vii]

The experiences I had with *Lolita* were different in quality and kind from the experiences I would have had, as a bartender in Galway, reading the same book. At the university, I was encouraged to seek out and apply a wider, more thoughtful, context to the reading experience. The insights I arrived at may not have been better than what I could have arrived at on my own, without the structure provided by the university, but the insights came much more readily at the university, where there were built-ins designed to encourage a particular kind of dialogue, a particular kind of critical thinking with others. At the university, I could learn by the listening and writing and speaking that complemented my solitary reading experience. My liberal education—in the form of four years spent at a university—helped me to get to the intellectual place I may have reached, on my own and without the infrastructure provided by the university, in twenty years.

The small entanglements created by volunteering, interning, and socializing made it harder for me to leave. And, once it became harder to leave, some of the magic of the academic environment could work on me. Not all the time. Not at every class meeting. Not during every lecture or discussion. Not while writing every essay or short story or poem. Certainly not while designing every PowerPoint presentation. But, here and there, I'd feel it: a little spark, the electricity of an idea coursing through me.

To realize the myriad benefits of a college education—economic, civic, intellectual—I think it's helpful to get a little entangled, to let the place *work* on you, to change you, to become a part of your life that's hard to shake loose. Even those who don't consider themslves "joiners" should do these sorts of activities—joining organizations, volunteering, pursuing the ideas of the classroom outside of the classroom—so that they have, if nothing else, a few more obstacles to quitting, a few more entries on the "cons" list, a few more people who'd be bummed if they left.

For me, the reason that trumps the civic and economic benefits of a college education, though those aren't negligible, is what a liberal education at a college can do for the intellects, maybe even the souls, of most of us in the vast middle of the bell curve of intellectual life. At their best, colleges and universities that provide liberal educations also provide an infrastructure for students, many of whom are at the crucial juncture between adolescence and adulthood, to investigate big ideas, to perform explorations into what has been and what is possible in the mind and world.

Even if we don't agree—or especially since we don't agree—about what's the best of what's been thought and said, universities must give their residents, students and teachers alike, opportunities to investigate, to write, to read, to inquire into what those ideas are and what might be those ideas' continuing relevance in our lives.

In an interview in *The Believer*, short-story writer George Saunders talks about the value of pursuing advanced study in creative writing, despite the practical difficulties presented by the modern publishing environment for literary fiction and poetry:

> Even for those thousands of young people who don't [publish], the process is still a noble one—the process of trying to say something, of working through craft issues and the worldview issues and the ego issues—all of this is character-building, and, God forbid, everything we do should have concrete career results. I've seen time and time again the way that the process of trying to say something dignifies and improves a person.[viii]

What a lovely sentiment: *the process of trying to say something dignifies and improves a person.* There are other kinds of work, beyond "trying to say something," that might also dignify and improve a person, and many of those other kinds of work are features of a liberal education. If the students engaged in a course of study leave slightly better able to say something, slightly better able to ask questions of significance, slightly better able to investigate the ideas that seem to matter, then maybe it's worth all the cost and effort.

We may not all agree on what counts as a "big idea." What might be a big idea for a first-year college student interested in geology may not resonate with the fifth-year student pursuing a degree in philosophy. Perhaps you've read *Lolita*, and you can't sympathize with my reactions; maybe you think my thesis is bunk. But maybe we can agree that, whatever ideas are being pursued in college, that pursuit should more often than not dignify and improve the pursuer.

Alongside asking big questions and searching after big answers, a college or university may also give its students opportunities to learn skills, aptitudes and even bits of knowledge that might be useful in their various future careers. To adapt the old adage, we can teach students how to fish. But I'd argue that, while teaching students to fish, while encouraging them to develop the aptitudes and abilities that will help them maintain and improve their livelihoods, colleges and universities—if they're going to be more than vocational credentialing services—must also ask students big questions, put them in positions where they have to ruminate over big ideas, to think and write and speak about justice, beauty, and truth, about what might be the features of the good life.[ix]

It's no small question: What's the university for? And it's exactly the kind of question that universities, when they're doing their best work, can engage in and provide forums—in writing, in speaking, in art, in inquiry—in which students participate. In the range of legitimate answers, however provisional, that we can provide can be found, too, an equally impressive range of implications for economies of the household and the nation, for the individual soul, and for the communities that we live in and hope to create.

Elizabeth Stephan
1993 Alumnus

I Regret Nothing

I arrived at Northwest in the August of 1988. I left May 1993. I was 18 when I arrived, and I was terrified. I think most of us were terrified. I chose Northwest for many reasons. It was close enough to home that I could get there if I needed to but far enough away that it was, you know, away. I didn't know anyone there. It wasn't very expensive. I had no clue what I was getting myself into. I had no clue how much Maryville and Northwest would change my life.

I have more stories to tell than could fill a book. I experienced more than I can remember. But one of the things I learned the most from was getting suspended after my freshman year. That's what happens when you stop going to class.

Shortly after I arrived in Maryville, I went through orientation. I sat through lots of sessions that blended together. I did all the things I was supposed to do. What do I remember the most? Seeing a cute guy, walking up to him, and introducing myself. It isn't something I would normally do, but one of my best friends had made the trip to Maryville with me and she talked me into it. My friend left a few days later and it was just me. That guy? He became a good friend, and I eventually met other friends through him. His little house just off campus became our social gathering place for the year. Those friends? That guy? I lost touch with him years ago for many different reasons. But the people I met through him or because of him? They are still some of my best friends.

That one little encounter set up a huge part of my college career: my circle of friends. I wouldn't have stayed in Maryville if it hadn't been for them. Twenty-five years later, my life is better because of them.

It's starting to sound idyllic, isn't it? Parts of it were. I had lots of fun. Serious fun. I met so many people. I experienced and did things I had never imagined I could or would do. My college experience was kind of what is portrayed in movies, although they may not have been the best role models. See, while I was having fun I stopped going to class.

I know, it's not the type of thing your parents want you to read or that some want you to know about. But it happened. Looking back, I don't know why I stopped. I had signed up for a bunch of 8:00 a.m. classes. High school had started earlier, so why should 8:00 a.m. be so bad? It was so bad. And when you don't go to class, you kind of fail your classes. And I did. Big time. By midterms I was in a hole so big, I saw no way out. I was put on academic probation.

I had planned on doing better my second semester. I did, but not better enough. I was put on academic suspension. Basically, I had been kicked out for a semester. I wanted back in. During my second semester, I took a Medieval Humanities class that I loved. I had always liked history, but this was the only class I cared about and the only class I studied for. Just when I found a topic I could get passionate about, I was suspended.

I began asking questions and talking to my professors. I had to examine what I wanted from my life. I had to ask myself a lot of questions. After exploring all of my options, I petitioned for readmission and won. There were certain stipulations I was supposed to meet, but I don't remember what they were. However, I do know my GPA never fell below a 3.0 after that and rarely went below a 3.5. I went from being a lazy student to a diligent student. I loved being challenged. I loved to debate. I loved college.

I started Northwest as an art major, but graduated with a B.A. in History. I also knew that higher education was the place I wanted to spend my life. My intention was to teach history at a college level. I didn't, and I'm not. But I am an academic librarian and faculty at a mid-sized state university. I work with students both one-on-one and in the classroom. I love working with them, because I remember what it was like. I remember the good and the bad.

I've told many of them about my college experience. I tell them I screwed up, but I also tell them that I regret none of it.

And I don't. Why? I had a lot of fun. That may not be what I should say, but it's true. I learned a lot about myself. I learned what I wanted, and I learned how to look at a problem (my suspension) and come up with a solution. In the end, isn't that what college is about?

The other thing I tell them? You're young. While you may screw up so badly that you think you have ruined your life, you probably haven't. You are young and you can recover. Don't stop and don't give up.

Don't get me wrong. All that fun I had? I continued to have fun after I got serious, but I learned how to balance my social life with my academic life. I'll also admit that my social life was almost as important to me as my classes.

Listen, I could keep going and tell more stories, but I won't. What I want you, the reader, to take away from this is that the smallest things can change your life. At the same time, what may seem like the biggest problems, mistakes, or screw ups often aren't. My words of advice would be to meet new people. Have fun, but not too much fun. Ask questions, even if you feel stupid asking those questions. Make mistakes; if you aren't making mistakes you aren't trying new things. Don't be afraid to fail; you aren't perfect and you never will be. Failing is part of life and you will learn more from it than you could ever know.

Alyssa Striplin
Senior

The Loudmouth Begins

The biggest mistake I made in college was coming in with the expectation that I didn't need to make friends. I came to Northwest with a few of my best friends from my hometown, and I figured that was enough to get me through the next four years of my life. Making friends has never been easy for me, and I was lucky enough to have the handful I had my freshman year. I'm a creature of comfort, and the people I had with me made me comfortable enough to believe that I didn't really need to focus on socializing and meeting new people. I could focus on school, getting good grades, earn my degree in English and enjoy the people I already had around me when I could. I felt like they were the only ones who enjoyed me for the obnoxious loudmouth that I am, and I didn't have to hide my eccentricities from them. My friends pushed me to meet the new people they had met, but I kept my distance. I would go to class and not talk to anyone, not even people who tried to talk to me. I didn't want to put in the effort to meet new people because I was afraid to put myself out there and be ostracized for my quirks like I was in high school.

My anxiety about being social and being an outcast was a bundle of bad memories and habits that I wasn't trying to forget. I didn't understand that college is different and it's supposed to change people. It's all about opening you up to new experiences to shape you into the person you could become or wanted to be. However, I've never been one to embrace change, and I liked what I already had at the time. I learned the hard way that even though I was comfortable with where I was, the people who made me comfortable were not. The friends I had come to college with were growing up and apart from me. They had opened up, embraced the new, and found out that they didn't fit at Northwest like I did. They had different aspirations and were just being held back the longer they were here. I won't lie either. I pushed them to stay, which was selfish, and I'd give anything to take that back now. But I knew that if they left, I would be alone and it would be my own fault. So when they did leave, all at the same time, before the beginning of my junior year at school, I was devastated and felt like the rest of my college experience would be a lot lonelier and quieter.

As my junior year started, I decided I needed something to keep me busy. Something that would distract me and keep my mind off of the mass exodus that had occurred only a few months before. I was too scared to join any organizations or clubs that involved meeting new people, so I settled for applying for a job on campus. One of the people my friends had tried to get me to hang out with decided to help and said that he knew someone who worked at the Writing Center and knew they were hiring. He had told her about me and they both felt I'd make a great writing tutor. I applied nervously and was hired, although I was not very confident in my ability to work one-on-one with students and other tutors with no real experience tutoring, let alone interacting with people. I could talk, sure, but never in a way that wasn't silly, snarky and downright annoying at times. I wasn't sure I'd be able to handle the professional conversations I'd be having, not just with students, but the other tutors as well. I was worried my habit of being quiet around new people and not making friends would make working in the Writing Center a miserable experience.

I can still remember how tight my stomach was on my first day, walking up to the second floor of the library and anxiously approaching the glass windows of the Writing Center. I could see people inside, some that I recognized but no one that I felt comfortable around. I said my quiet hellos, sat in a chair off to the side and tried to get myself ready to tutor my first few students. There were so many degrees of discomfort. I felt like I was going to pass out in my chair. I can't explain why, but when I first met my co-workers, they intimidated me. Most of them were graduate students and they all seemed to have been working together for a long time. I was scared to ask them questions about what to expect with my students or what to say, but when I did finally muster up the courage I was surprised to find how kind they were. They didn't scoff at me or my seemingly silly questions about basic tutoring. Instead, they eagerly answered all my questions and offered strong words of encouragement that helped keep my spirits up through slow and uneasy sessions. Tutoring gradually got easier and I became more confident with my students, but I was still quiet and reserved around the office.

My fellow tutors, even the newer ones like myself at the time, tried their best to get me to open up whenever I was in the office. They tried to include me in their conversations, asked for my opinion on things and tried to get me to talk about my interests. At one point, they even had a "mandatory questionnaire" that everyone answered including questions about your favorite books, comics, movies, and superpowers. These people clearly weren't the kind to be excluding, and they seemed genuinely interested in getting to know me. The more time I spent around them, the more I became interested in them as well. The Writing Center seemed to be full of animated characters, confident in who they were, and I couldn't help but envy them. They were a talkative bunch too. Their conversations were always lively and I liked to eavesdrop on them because most of the time they were funny and about the things I was interested in. I'd make the occasional comment in a conversation about Harry Potter, add my opinion about the new Elder Scrolls game and tell a quick joke about Batman before returning to my wallflower position in the corner. I was never confident enough to include myself fully, but I could feel my voice getting louder every time I chimed in.

I can only describe what happened next as a scientific phenomenon, mostly because I want to avoid any "blossoming" metaphors. The longer I worked at the Writing Center, the more I felt pulled in by this immense gravitational pull that surrounded the people working there. Like a lonely little asteroid lost in space, I was suddenly becoming a part of a solar system. It wasn't against my will either. The other tutors were the people I needed to get me talking, the kind that I wanted to be friends with. They were smart, funny, confident and so warm and welcoming that they broke through my silent, stone-faced façade. Every time they laughed at my stupid jokes, offered me friendly advice, invited me to hang out, brought me to dinner or listened to me for a few minutes, the more I felt myself changing. They were the Batman to my Robin, taking me under their wing after a tragic happenstance and training me to become my own brand of hero. My voice was louder in conversations, noise-complaint loud, but it was my way of becoming a presence in the office and around campus. I was speaking up in class, showing off my new found abilities of speech like a rehabilitated mockingbird. Throughout the day, I'd always look forward to going to work and actually joining in on the conversations without being asked.

I wouldn't say this behavior was a sign of a "new" me. Instead it was a reinvigorated, bigger, louder and uncut version of my old self. When I talked in class, it wasn't just to hear the sound of my own voice. I was participating in discussions, offering my own viewpoint to others and enjoying my newly acquired skills of articulating my thoughts. Creative writing workshops and literature classes were my favorite, and I started to feel confident in my major again. I was becoming more integrated in the Colden Hall community, not just with students but faculty as well. Professors were remembering my name and the person behind it, not just as the loudmouth that disrupts their classes on occasion, but as a bright, young woman with passion and a smidge of talent. New opportunities were opening up for me, like internships and classes that helped solidify my passion for writing and a future career in publishing and being published. All of these accomplishments came without me hiding my personality from anyone. I had made new friends, fellow tutors and classmates, who appreciated who I was and who I greatly appreciated in return.

As I stand on the verge of graduating and entering graduate school, I can happily say that junior year was not as miserable as I had first imagined. I would go so far as to say it was my favorite time in college so far. It was a time where I learned to be more receptive to the people around me and take full advantage of the experiences at my fingertips. If I hadn't turned in the job application for the Writing Center, I don't think I would be the person I am now. I'd be alone in a dorm somewhere, quietly lamenting about a wasted college experience. Instead, I'm enjoying new friends, taking my first steps towards graduate school and eventually an M.F.A. program to invest in my future as a writer. I'm also continuing my work at the Writing Center, making friends with new tutors and saying goodbye to those that helped me the most. The new tutors that read this story probably have trouble wrapping their heads around the concept that at one point I was quiet and reserved. All I can say to them is that the loudmouth rises, and she's never going away again.

Helen Strotman
Junior

Beauty Inveterate

In his classic play *Our Town*, Thornton Wilder wrote: "We all know something is eternal. And that something has to do with human beings."[i] (For those of you, and I know there are many of you, who are groaning at the *Our Town* reference, hang on tight—little do you know, you're the object of a case study.) In the spring of 2011, Theatre Northwest produced *Our Town* on the Mary Linn stage directed by Dr. Joe Kreizinger, and I was lucky enough to be cast in the role of Emily Webb. Now, I'll just put this out there now to avoid any confusion: I love *Our Town*. I find it to be one of the greatest and most important plays in the American theatrical canon, and I rank Thornton Wilder very high on my personal list of favorite playwrights. Oddly enough, however, the number of people I've found who loathe *Our Town* outnumber those who love it nearly ten to one. In fact, I get almost identical reactions from those around me when I express my love and enjoyment of this play: "Ew. What?! *Our Town*? Gross. That play is horrible. I hate it. What is wrong with you?"

The first time I heard that it was hard—almost spirit crushing. I was a young theatre artist who loved a work that, and this is a fact that cannot be argued, is one of the most popular, most widely produced plays in the United States. And although I understand and respect the fact that not everyone is going to like everything, and that people have a perfectly legitimate right not to find *Our Town* as poignant as I do, I never expected such a harsh attack to come spiraling at me. I didn't know how to combat that. So I started to animate my love for it, make it almost melodramatic to the point that it was nearly a joke. I figured that if I portrayed my love of this text in a way that was almost nostalgic, slightly quirky, then the insults from my friends would take the form of witty banter and I couldn't be seriously disheartened.

But I was.

It was around this same time in my life, my freshman year of college, that I began to hear, through various media outlets and conversations, that the world was "devoid of beauty." I didn't get it. At this point in my life I was doe-eyed, I looked at the world through rose-colored glasses. I didn't like the idea that beauty was disappearing from the world, so I looked for the beauty in everything from *Our Town* to William Faulkner to *How I Met Your Mother*. And I could find it if I looked hard enough. And I was content.

And then my grandmother got cancer.

It was the first semester of my freshman year, and my cousin was getting married in Iowa. I was unable to go, however, because I was in a play opening that weekend. I called my grandma and asked her if she was excited for the wedding, but she said that she was sick and that she and my grandfather weren't going to go. And then my father called and said, "You know it's cancer, right?" I didn't know, of course, because he hadn't told me. But it was cancer, and she started chemo and we waited. That Thanksgiving nearly my entire family went down to their tiny house in Rockwall, Texas, and we celebrated and laughed, and it was beautiful.

And as we said our goodbyes my cousin told my sister that our grandpa also had developed cancer. But it wasn't as serious as Grandma's, and I pushed it to the back of my mind and tried to keep those rose-colored glasses from slipping. I planned another visit to Texas for spring break, telling my grandma that I wanted to come down and help out around the house. The plan was that I would go and sit with her during her chemo, because none of my aunts would be able to be there that week. But Grandma went into remission, and Grandpa felt great. So, instead of doctors' offices we went to see both *The King's Speech* and *The Lincoln Lawyer* in one week, Gram took me shopping, and they surprised me with tickets to a Horton Foote play at the Dallas Theater Center, and everything was perfect.

But the cancer came back, as it always seems to, and I began to wonder. I wondered about the concept of a world being devoid of beauty. Maybe it was true. I didn't understand. I didn't understand how people who were eighty years old could die of cancer, but murderers could live forever. So I smashed my rose-colored glasses into the dust, and I became a quiet, closeted cynic. I stopped looking for beauty and began to notice the world only for the things it took from us. But the one thing that never seemed to fade was *Our Town*. At my lowest points of despair and internal agony that play would pop into my mind like a firework. Wilder wrote: "We all know that something is eternal." "What," I kept asking myself, day after day. "What is eternal?" In the world around me, all I could see was suffering. Suffering was eternal. Suffering and pain, agony and torment, horror and anger. I know this all seems melodramatic, but it was honestly how I felt for nearly two years.

But in the fall of 2012, a year and a half after my grandmother's cancer had come back with a vengeance, I began my junior year of college. I sat in my theatre history classroom and listened to a lecture on Eastern Theatre and how the decorum of the time required that everything performed be aesthetically pleasing. It had to be beautiful. In my head, I thought, "Well then, lots of made up stories about perfect worlds where no one gets cancer." And then my professor explained something that threw my perception for a loop: "You can still depict the grotesque, as long as it is done in a beautiful way. For example: crying on stage is not beautiful, so we find a symbolic way to show that a character is crying, while still creating an aesthetically beautiful image."

I spent the entire night thinking about that concept, the concept of a world, a style, where some of the most unbeautiful things must be depicted in a beautiful way. And then, as it tends to do, my mind circled back to *Our Town* and the image of George kneeling next to Emily's grave at the end of act three, broken over the loss of his one true love. Death and loss aren't beautiful, but here they were depicted in a beautiful way. The next morning I woke up and the world was a little more rose-colored. I took my copy of *Our Town* with me, re-reading it and letting the familiar words unfold with new meaning, with new beauty.

But people still gave me shit for liking it. A friend of mine looked at me and said "Oh, Helen's reading *Our Town,* the worst play ever written." I braced myself for the familiar weight of despair that came with such a taunting comment. But before the despair struck, something else hit me: the world seems to be devoid of beauty because we, as humans, inherently destroy it for each other. We mock the places where others find beauty, because if there is beauty in something that we don't understand, we fear it. We feel the subconscious need to destroy it so that the things in which we find beauty remain sacred. And this wasn't just a case of people picking on me for my literary tastes. We all do it, every single day. You hear someone say, "I love Paramore," and you roll your eyes and laugh because you think that their music is the worst shit to have ever been recorded. But you never stop to think that that person who loves Paramore sees in it a beauty that you miss, or that you don't understand simply because it's not the beauty you find poignant and prevalent.

We all do this. This isn't an essay crying out for everyone to be nice and stop making fun of each other. If we didn't have differing opinions, we wouldn't be able to elicit change or have intriguing conversations. We have the power to form and voice opinions for a reason. But one of the most important things I have learned in my three years as a college student is that beauty is important. At Northwest, we're surrounded by beauty: our beautiful campus, the paintings hanging in the Fine Arts building, the hand-made dresses in Theatre Northwest's costume shop, the moment of triumph when a science experiment yields the result you've been waiting for. What I've learned, what it all boils down to, is that the things we find beautiful are precious. They are what make us who we are, and they are what get us through the most difficult parts of our lives.

My grandmother passed away on December 29, 2012. She was eighty years old. She died in her home, with her husband (whom she'd known since first grade) and all six of her children there to bid her goodbye. When I found out, I lost the beauty for a moment; loss and grief tend to eclipse it in situations like that. But we went down to Texas, her vigil and funeral were filled to the brim with people who loved her, who cared for her, who found her presence in their lives beautiful. So even though I had to sing a heartbreaking farewell song to the most important woman in my life, even though I had to stare out at the grief-stricken faces of my family, all of it was beautiful. It was beautiful, because as I sang through tears I looked out on my grandmother's lasting legacy: her husband, her sister, her six children and her sixteen grandchildren. She might have left us, but she left the world filled with beauty, and people to find and create and cultivate it.

And then I realized what's eternal.

**Clayton Stuart
Senior**

The Zoo

People don't often think of joining a fraternity as joining a home. They think of it as "paying for friends," "an excuse to drink," or any other stereotype that has arisen because only the bad things get remembered. To me, as well as countless others, my fraternity's house, our beliefs, my brothers… that is my home.

What makes it a home? Well that's pretty simple, it's where I have enjoyed, loved, hated, continued, quit, fought, and lived. I have done a lot of things during college because of my fraternity and I wouldn't change my experience for any other. Living in a house with 16 other people is a challenge. There are things that go wrong, but that gives us the opportunity to work together to solve them. People ask me how it is being in a fraternity and a lot of the time I give one answer: it's a zoo.

Every fraternity has some form of an executive board. Ours is comprised of our President, Vice President, Treasurer, Sergeant at Arms, and Secretary. These are members that have earned the respect of their brothers and were voted into each office respectfully. They are the ones in charge and have a lot of responsibility for keeping the chapter under control. The upperclassmen often take a similar role in the responsibility of helping keep the chapter under control. The executive board and upperclassmen are the zookeepers.

Next up are the brothers in charge of the entertainment of the chapter. These are the members who, even though you expect it, do something that will either piss you off or make you laugh. These guys are the ones that you need to keep an eye on. The moment you look away these guys are shaving an eyebrow when you're sleeping, taking a slice of pizza you just ordered, putting a motorized vehicle in the bathroom, or bugging you to play video games while you're studying. These are the monkeys. Every member at some point will do something to earn them this title. Without these guys the zoo would be boring.

Not every member is able to live in the house at the same time; a lot of guys have their own houses or apartments away from the house. Usually upperclassmen, these guys still always pop in whenever they feel like it. You never quite know when these guys are going to stop in for a visit. Some visit more than others. These guys are the geese that fly in and out of the zoo. When they're around you chase them through the zoo, but when they're not around then there's still plenty to do.

Just like in a zoo, there are always younger people running around trying to figure out what this whole thing is about. They are the ones trying to learn as much as possible about the fraternity that they're in. These younger guys are the visiting field trip of elementary school kids. They are the fraternity's new members. They're running around the zoo with their chaperones, our new member educators, trying to visit every exhibit and learn as much as they can. The new member educators are there to pull them back on track when they start to get into trouble or do something they shouldn't do. Eventually these members will find their way to something that they wish they could be—a zookeeper, monkey, or something else—and they will stay there. Eventually becoming part of the zoo and assuming a new role.

There are always a few guys that will never serve on the executive board and that's completely okay. These are the guys that might not be the one in charge of an event, but they're always there to help out and do what is asked of them. These guys are like the petting zoo. The animals in the petting zoo aren't the big attraction, but they are essential to the zoo-goers' experience. These guys will be there when you need them and will do what is needed.

As in anything though, everyone moves on to something bigger. Animals change in the zoo and those kids on the field trip eventually become the donors for the zoo to keep it running. Our alumni are those donors. They are still part of the zoo, but their participation has taken a much different role. They donate money to keep the zoo going and are always there to offer insight as to how things could become better. They also come back during homecoming or for other reasons to relive their days in which they might have been a monkey or a zookeeper.

I'll never be able to put the full fraternity experience into words. It is simply one thing that some must go through firsthand in order to understand it. There is a reason that this select group of guys are called my brothers. They are the ones that I have shared my experiences with. They are the ones that have given me a home that I will never be able to leave. It just so happens that my home . . . is a zoo.

Richard Toomey
Associate Professor, Natural Sciences

Subjectivity, Objectivity and the Value of a University Education

I tend to see the world in black and white. At times, my discipline demands it, and I find myself struggling constantly to convey to my students the need to remove the biases that they bring to their analysis of cold, implacable numbers. In my world there are only measurements, speculation, equations, and statistics. Nature offers little in the way of latitude when it comes to interpretation. Simply put, the equations either accurately model what it shows us or they don't. There is no good. There is no bad. Nothing is benevolent. Nothing is malign. Everything simply "is." The goal of my discipline is to poke and prod nature until it allows me a glimpse into how the universe behaves under the pretense that I, that we, are not part of it; therein lies the dilemma. How does one effectively teach objectivity to himself or to his students? The scientific method is the cornerstone of practical, objective practices, but how does one educate others about the nature of science when the means by which we communicate requires us to collapse upon the reality that we, as part of nature, are inherently subjective.

As a science educator, it is my responsibility to teach students the difference between subjectivity and objectivity and how the former is to be removed, as effectively as can be, to foster unbiased discovery. I have been charged with training individuals in a lab to see the world in a way that is very different from the world in which they otherwise live. I have the task of facilitating their mastery of balance, if not harmony, that is necessary between the unfeeling scrutiny of the material world and the creativity that drives exploration and inquiry.

I once had a very engaging, very bright, and very socially inept science major ask me to justify why the university was "forcing" him to "waste his time and money" taking courses in the humanities and arts, when all he wanted to study was science and mathematics. It was the first time I had been asked the question so directly, and, for a moment, I wanted to confide in him that, years ago, I shared the same perspective. I am sure that I was no more eloquent then as I am now with my response, but it was something along the lines of: "What do you value?" I don't think it was until then that I truly understood what the university represented and what its purpose really was, even though I had spent almost half of my life within its walls. In whatever context you choose to see it, we walk the top of the fence between the subjective and objective parts of human experience. The purpose of the university, the purpose of a university education, is to offer us a means of gaining perspective on the balance between the two. As much as we want to convince ourselves that our sense of equilibrium is fine and that we know how to function from day to day, I would argue that the skill set, vision, and mental cultivation, provided to us by the myriad and often imperceptible influences we are exposed to daily from institutions such as Northwest, force us to wake up different people today than we were yesterday.

I may be a scientist who strives for objectivity in both my teaching and my research, but I do not exist alone in the universe. My sister disciplines continually make me appreciate how I have come to revere and cherish the people and ideologies that define me as a member of society and a lifelong learner. The esteem of the subjectivity of a university education is that in seeing how others live and have lived and in seeing how others express themselves through literature, the arts, philosophy, culture, mythology and religion, we are able to gain perspective on what constitutes "our" values, on what it is that we, as individuals, families, communities, and a species, embrace as meaningful. They don't have to be ubiquitous or appealing, but they are ours. We earn them through interaction, through triumph and suffering. They encompass how we invest our emotions, and they reflect themselves in how we treat ourselves and others. They serve as the cornerstone of the morals of our greater commonwealth, the pillars of our professional ethics, and our collective sense of social justice. And to scientists, they give meaning to our endeavors.

My colleagues and I in the STEM (Science, Technology, Engineering, and Mathematics) disiciplines try to convey to our students the grandeur, wonder, awe, and sense of insignificance that we, as entities in the universe, are privy to as it, in both large and small scale, opens doors that lead to continual discovery. I would postulate that it is the role of my colleagues in the complementary disciplines, across the university, to teach our students how to hone their understanding, if not mastery, of the subjectivity of the self and the subjectivity of the many. How to look, not only with sight but with substance, into the universe and its machinations, and find our particular place in it. How to express our thoughts and emotions in ways that both anger us and incite tears. How to exist with ourselves and how to coexist with one another. The purpose of the university is to show us that we never truly stop being susceptible to external, relentless influences that alter our environments as we live our lives, even when the university experience is over.

Tim Pawlenty, a former Governor of Minnesota and presidential candidate, once declared on a talk show that (to paraphrase) there was no need to pay thousands of dollars to have America's children sit in a lecture hall and listen to a boring professor when they can have the same lecture delivered to them, efficiently and economically, through their iPods. I would challenge that gentleman to place the average, freshman, or even himself, in isolation with the textbooks or, even better, an iPod loaded with the lectures required to earn a degree, and, in four years, demonstrate the proficiency that is justifiably expected.

To devalue the university experience and the central role it plays in our education in life, by equating face-to-face interaction with an audio-only delivery, is flat-out insulting. Lecturing is dead and most of us are aware of that. To devalue the importance of the Socratic dialogue in its contribution towards creating individuals capable of independent thought is a travesty and illustrates a complete lack of what we, as educators, strive to do every day. The irony that I find in this is that the very technology that the aforementioned individual espouses is, I believe, partly to blame. The need for instant gratification and the readily available transmission of information has, to some degree, ruined the beauty of the spoken and written word. It has removed people's ability to resolve conflict and rendered face-to-face communication an annoyance. When the expression of oneself devolves into misspelled words on a 3-inch screen, the need for re-evaluating the purpose of a university is as important as it may have ever been.

I will conclude with two contrasting examples of why there is a purpose to a university education.

In May 2007, ten men who were seeking the office of President of the United States were asked if they "believed" in the theory of evolution; three of them claimed they did not. I cannot convey to you how disappointed I am that the future leaders of this nation, if not any nation, are incapable of learning the meaning of the words they use. Given the depth to which science, medicine, engineering, and technology pervade our daily lives, we need to be educated enough to recognize that words misused are just as, if not more, formidable than words that are well thought out. The objectivity of the scientific method leads to conclusions that are not subject to any one's belief systems. A scientific theory is no more beholden to a person's "beliefs" than those very same beliefs are beholden to the rules of evidence. However, just because fruits of scientific endeavors are without ethic, their applications are not. In a university, a student can gain the insight and understanding that would allow them to recognize that distinction.

On February 28, 1998, *The Lancet* published an article written by a group of 13 scientists, of whom the PI, or principal investigator, was Andrew Wakefield, that linked the MMR vaccination and autistic phenotypes in previously "normal" children. In a press conference held prior to publication of the article, Wakefield suggested a suspension of the MMR vaccine until more studies could be done, even though the article itself suggested insufficient statistical weight to make an ethical claim. *The Lancet*, and all the authors but Wakefield, retracted their claim to the paper in 2004, a day before the press reported that the children in the study were chosen by a lawyer who was preparing to sue MMR vaccine manufacturers and that the study's funding was paid by said lawyers who also paid Wakefield approximately $500,000 to conduct the research. Graduate students of Wakefield's testified that he intentionally rejected data that did not support his hypothesis. Since then, proper, statistically significant studies have been conducted by independent laboratories, all of whom found no link between autism, measles, and vaccinations. Sadly, retractions that are not on the front page are not as sensational or lucrative as those that catch one's eye, even if they are more informative, more accurate, and ethical. As a scientist, Dr. Wakefield should have known better than to prey upon our fears. In a university, a student can learn the ethics of science, of community, of life. In a university a student can ask and learn how to answer the question: Just because you can, should you?

When I was a child my father used to look with awe upon the men and women he believed to be "Renaissance," hoping some day to be perceived by others as such. Those people, he believed, were students of the world. I believe, at its core, that is the purpose of the university education, to make us all students of the world.

Mara Wilson
Senior

Finishing the Book

When I start reading a book I always finish it. I don't know when I began this custom for myself, but even if the book is awful, even if I absolutely cannot stand it, I will finish it. It may take me a lot longer than usual to finish the book, with frequent breaks or reading a paragraph every week or skimming the long paragraphs or just leaving it alone for a while. Ultimately once I begin reading a book it becomes a personal goal to make it through and complete it. Every time I pick the book back up I think if I can just get through this one page, these two chapters, I'll be that much closer to being done with it. *Life of Pi* took me about three years of off and on reading to complete. I began *Cold Mountain* my junior year of high school and I've yet to get past page 75. I've wanted to give up on reading this and many other books before, but for some reason I can't bring myself to. Sometimes when I finally reach a book's end I'm disappointed, but on a rare occasion I find I'm surprised by the ending and my perspective has shifted for the better. *Pride and Prejudice* was this way for me, as was *The Host* and even one of my all-time favorites, *The Count of Monte Cristo*.

It's a little less than two months away from graduation and I can't help but think my college career is similar to my goal of finishing every book I begin. I didn't want to go college in the first place. When I finally decided to go, I applied to four schools and was accepted into all of them, University of Omaha (I'm from Nebraska), Doane College, California State University at Fullerton, and here at Northwest Missouri State University. I toured Cal State Fullerton's campus and Northwest's. I'll admit I let my sister influence my decision to go to Northwest. She was an alumnus and had the best time of her life while in college. I also couldn't bring myself to move that far from home, even though I loved the campus at Cal

State. Northwest was my choice. Since freshman year I've been convinced college is a corporate, money-sucking establishment focused on an unrealistic idea of trying to cram information into students' heads in order to prepare them for their future careers, and where, once they graduate, they may or may not land a job. There are a lot of "ifs" and "maybes," and as much as college prepares you over the four or more years you're there it's ultimately up to you, once you graduate, to decide what to do next with your life. One of the scariest parts about college is getting out of it. Even though that's all I seemed to want to do for the last three and a half years. I didn't want to be in college, but I definitely wasn't ready and am still not ready to be out of it and make a decision about where I want to be in the "real world."

Up until this last week, when I began writing this paper, I had believed that a university was a complete waste of time. Not only due to the corporate-money-sucking theory but based on the idea of taking general education courses, along with your major course work. Your major is what you want to do with your life, so why wouldn't you want to focus your time solely on the skills you'll need to know before you graduate for your career? Why would you like being forced to take courses that expose and in some cases immerse you in numerous different genres of study? We are a modern and constantly expanding society. We are seen as people who want freedom, to broaden our minds and learn all we can because we are young and vibrant. Taking courses outside of our own major seems like such a bad idea and a waste of time, but is it really? Do we want to restrict ourselves to only one major and one subject matter? If yes, then how do you explain many students with double majors and minors or students who have changed their major more than once? Taking classes like biology or historical fiction, which I had just taken in high school, seemed like a waste of my time. This part of getting the university degree may seem pointless, but really it's all part of the experience.

For example, my decision to switch to an English major was tough for me at first because I had convinced myself that theatre was my path, until I looked back at my life and realized theatre and performing had always been a hobby, but writing and reading was my true passion. Something I had always had a natural creative ability for. I never would've found this out without taking my two English general education courses. The first being Composition, with a teacher that has shifted my perspective in my own writing multiple times and taught me more than I can ever thank him for. The second class was Introduction to Literature with a teacher who asked if I was an English major (at the time I was not) and through her comments on my papers suggested that I would be an excellent candidate for the major. I realized she was right. I talked to my advisor about switching and the rest of my college career has been the best experience I ever could have asked for.

I'm the student that hates maximum page limits on papers and struggles to cut things (this document proves that). This past year, through my English courses, internship and yearbook experience, I've learned that editing is actually a tremendously helpful device and it is now where I want to move forward in my life and with my career. Switching my major was the best decision I could have made, and I may not have figured this without going to college, coming to this university specifically, and taking those "pointless" general education courses.

When you put a large group of diverse individuals in one place, in one room, you are going to get a series of situations and experiences. The university experience not only mixes up our own thoughts and ideas, but it allows us to hear others' and think through them together. It diversifies us in a way we could not get in any other setting. I've learned a lifetime of information and experiences I couldn't have gotten without being on this campus and in the university atmosphere. I've seen and done things I may not have seen or done anywhere else. Through this I have grown, but that doesn't mean there weren't moments when I wanted to quit.

From freshman year up until now I have wanted to quit college more times than I could count, but I didn't. Sometimes it was because I knew my parents wouldn't let me, but the truth is they couldn't have stopped me if that's what I had really wanted to do. Ultimately it was my decision and I stayed, but why? When I was up until 5 a.m. finishing that theatre analysis freshman year or when I had to get up every morning at 7 a.m. to make it to the dreaded 8 o'clock classes, why didn't I just quit?

When you mix your life with college things get complicated. You're forced to make decisions you never thought you'd have to make. Going to class versus going to that concert I've wanted to go to for such a long time. I stayed up all night studying for one class, so I can sleep in through my first class right, or should I go? What about when I had a midterm the day after

St. Patrick's Day, but my roommates wanted me to go to the bars with them Saturday and Sunday night? When I knew I was going to fail my Spanish class because I hadn't been to class in over a week. There was snow above my ankle outside, but I still have class. Should I go? When that half of a page study guide turns into four pages as I fill it in and my stress level goes from low to high in a matter of seconds, why didn't I give up? I knew I wouldn't be able to learn all of that information in a few days anyway. The stakes are raised when you go to college out of state. The dog I've had since third grade was sick and they were going to have to put him down on a Friday, but I had class all day. When my boyfriend came in town on Thursday, should I stay with him Friday morning instead of going to my one class? My grandpa's funeral was on a Wednesday. My niece's birthday party was on a Tuesday. I was diagnosed with mono and had to miss class for almost a full two weeks. Why didn't I choose to take the semester off to recover?

Quitting would have been the easiest thing to do in any of these situations. But just like reading those books that are so difficult to get through, I have yet to quit. That doesn't mean I don't still have the desire to at times. With each and every decision I've listed here, it wasn't easy. There were times when I chose to sleep in. I went home to see my dog before he died. I celebrated my niece's two-year-old birthday that was on a Tuesday when I had class. I chose to have my own snow day, when the campus didn't. I went to that concert and I went out to the bar on a night I had an exam the next day. Sometimes I was rewarded for my breaks because I was rejuvenated and motivated to continue forth. Other times I was reprimanded for my decisions. I failed my Spanish class. I missed a review for an exam, and I received a C on that exam. Not all of these choices were the "right" ones, but they were mine to make and that is where I learned the most.

When making a decision I sometimes thought, if I go to this one class today, if I do these four assignments, if I study and ace this exam, I'll be one step closer to finishing. I'll be one step closer to achieving one of the most underestimated and difficult tasks: getting that degree. Although I've listed all of the moments where I made the wrong choice, I obviously made the good college student decisions as well or I wouldn't have gotten 4.0s in three of my semesters. I haven't quit. I am completing this chapter in my life, with a few breaks along the way. It's about balance, knowing when to give yourself a break and when to force yourself to push through. Knowing you're not always going to make the right decision, but it well help you learn what's good for you and you will grow through this. As long as you don't give up, that's what matters. Finish the book with an open mind and you might end up being surprised by what you've learned along the way and who you've become.

Notes

Richard Sonnenmoser, "Introduction"
i. Charles Tilly, *Why?* (2006), published by Princeton University Press, p. 64.

Kori Binette, "Time to Get Gritty: The Non-Academic Stuff That Makes You a Better Student"
i. Patrick Sullivan and David Nielsen, "'Ability to Benefit': Making Forward-Looking Decisions about Our Most Underprepared Students," published in *College English* 45.3 (January 2013), p. 325.

Amanda Petefish-Schrag, "An Education Worth Selling"
i. Eric Overmeyer, *On the Verge* (1986), published by Broadway Play Publishing.

ii. Richard Arum and Josipa Roksa, *Academically Adrift: Limited Learning on College Campuses* (2010), published by University of Chicago Press.

iii. From a February 18, 1989, editorial in *The Independent,* "Limit to Mutual Tolerance."

Richard Sonnenmoser, "Big Questions, Small Entanglements"
i. From 1998 to 2002, I was an undergraduate student at the University of Missouri. From 2002 to 2005, I worked in that same university's Office of Admissions. From 2005 to 2008, I was a graduate student and teaching associate at the University of Massachusetts Amherst, and from 2008 to the present I've taught courses in writing and literature at Northwest Missouri State University.

ii. The National Center for Education Statistics is part of the U.S. Department of Education. The statistics cited here are summarized from the "Condition of Education" report for 2012, which is available at nces.ed.gov.

iii. Matthew Arnold, "Preface," *Culture and Anarchy: An Essay in Political and Social Criticism* (1889), published by Smith, Elder and Co., p. *viii.* Arnold's definition of culture—"the best which has been thought and said in the world"—is often cited in discussions about the value of liberal education and the value of colleges and universities more generally. In his preface, Arnold writes, "The whole scope of the essay is to recommend culture as the great help out of our present difficulties; culture being a pursuit of our total perfection by means of getting to know, on all the matters which most concern us, the best which has been thought and said in the world, and, through this knowledge, turning a stream of fresh and free thought upon our stock notions and habits, which we now follow staunchly and mechanically, vainly imagining that there is a virtue in following them staunchly which makes up for the mischief of following them mechanically."

iv. I first saw the Strayer University advertisement on a cable television station in February 2013. While images of children and books and tools and baked goods play on screen, the voiceover intones: "You conquered this, read every one of these, built this out of these, even turned your kitchen into this. And any of those make this actually doable. We can help by giving you credit for things you've already done. So you can earn your degree for less time and money than you think. You're ready for Strayer University." The ad relies on the pairing of pronouns with visual antecedents. The words "you conquered this" coincide with the image of children running through a hallway and then standing on their heads on a sofa. "Read every one of these" is heard as viewers see an overflowing bookcase. We hear "built this out of these" while viewing images of an older, perhaps rebuilt, car and its constituent parts. "Even turned your kitchen into this" refers, it seems, to a home bakery business. The advertisement can be seen online at www.ispot.tv.

v. "College Inc.," an episode of the PBS series *Frontline*, written by John Maggio and Martin Smith, produced by Chris Durrance, John Maggio, and Martin Smith, originally broadcast on May 4, 2010. Transcript and video copies of "College Inc." are available at the *Frontline* website on pbs.org.

vi. The epigraph to this essay is quoted from Andrew Delbanco's *College: What is Was, Is, and Should Be* (2012), published by Princeton University Press, p. 171.

vii. It's difficult for me to imagine a college or university where people don't have the time or inclination or encouragement, however slight, to "sit down and think." (I'm fine, I should add, with the possibility of university denizens standing and thinking, if it suits them, or thinking while lying on a futon.)

viii. Ben Marcus's interview with George Saunders appears in the March 2004 issue of *The Believer*.

ix. A few books have undoubtedly influenced my thinking about what sorts of inquiries might be most necessary for college students: Andrew Delbanco's *College: What it Was, Is, and Should Be* (2012), published by Princeton University Press; Robert Skidelsky and Edward Skidelsky's *How Much is Enough?: Money and the Good Life* (2012), published by Other Press; and Mark Edmundson's *Why Read?* (2005), published by Bloomsbury USA.

Helen Strotman, "Beauty Invertate"

i. Thornton Wilder, *Our Town* (1938), published by Coward McCann.

Made in the USA
Lexington, KY
12 August 2019